Walking on the Earth

poems

Jamieson Wolf

This is a work of fiction. Names, characters, places, and incidents are products of the author's imagination or are used fictitiously and are not to be construed as real. Any resemblance to actual events, locales, organizations, or persons, living or dead, is entirely coincidental.

Walking on the Earth

Copyright© 2015 Jamieson Wolf

 ISBN: 978-1-928101-03-1

Cover Artist: Jamieson Wolf

Text: Jamieson Wolf

Wolf Flow Press

www.wolfflowpress.com

PRAISE FOR JAMIESON WOLF

"Jamieson Wolf is a gifted writer!"
Kelley Armstrong, New York Times Best Selling Author

"As I read, Jamieson Wolf taught me to dance to the beats of his heart. Tender, heartbreaking and beautiful."
Caroline Smailes, Author of In Search of Adam, Black Boxes, Like Bees to Honey and The Drowning of Arthur Braxton

"Jamieson Wolf writes like Augusten Burroughs without the cynicism."
Nasim Marie Jafry, Author of The State of Me

PRAISE FOR TALKING TO THE SKY

"Expect the unexpected and be pleasantly surprised. Keep an open mind and heart and travel along with this author on a journey through life. Experience with him just what he has been living with and through this last year. I challenge you to change your thinking and attitude with this book. Bring on the adventure as you travel with him and get Talking to the Sky yourself."
Elaine Breault

I have had the pleasure of reading this collection a few times and will many more I am sure. Jamieson's words provokes the entire spectrum of emotions in his words, allowing feelings to surface in the reader easily. There is an almost haunting permanence in the stories he weaves, one that has taken me to my own experiences that I thought were long lost. This poet is magical. His words are

powerful and loving. A very very good read!!
Dava Gamble, Author of Silver Journey's and Silver Cusp

"With his unique style and powerful imagery, Jamieson Wolf lures us into this beautiful volume of poetry. Colors splash across the page, emotions are captured in a single word or phrase. We ride the city bus and see a woman's tears, feel the touch of a caring hand, experience the joy in a child's smile.

We walk a city street, hushed with snow. Friends and lovers meet with a warm breath on the cheek, a kiss, a sad goodbye. We witness courage, personal growth, moments of humor, strength, snatches of a dream.

Each poem is a stolen moment in time, raw, vivid, and intimate. Touching the Sky is an uplifting affirmation of life not soon forgotten."
Dianne Harstock, Author of Alex, Without Aiden and Philips Watcher

For Michael

A Note About Walking on the Earth

The poems contained in Talking to the Sky helped me to find my voice again.

After months of staring at my computer screen, I was writing once more. No longer was I talking to the sky that couldn't hear me. Now the words were flowing. They became the next phase in my healing as I wrote to find myself again.

If Talking to the Sky was all about finding my voice again, Walking on the Earth is about the path I've taken and the choices I've made to living a better life. I look at all of the poems in Talking with the Earth like stepping stones along that path. Each poem is a marker of where I was, who I was with and what I accomplished.

There are a lot of people I'm thankful for coming with me along this path I'm on. This book is for them: WM and WD, Kimberlee, Karine, Nai, Laurie, Dava, Meaghan, Julie, Alexandra, Heather and Jackie and Dianne. My life would be less bright without you.

Really, though, this book is for Michael. You've changed my life and have taught me what it is to love and be loved in return. I don't have enough words to tell you what you mean to me, but hopefully the poems in this collection that I wrote for you will come close.

Jamieson

Amicus optima vitae possessio

I went to see a wise woman.
She looked at my palms
and read my cards.
She burned incense
and chanted, and asked
if she could read my aura.
I was anxious during all this,
the question I uttered
still burning my tongue.
Then the wise woman was still.
She looked at me and smiled,
one that reached her eyes
and filled me with a calmness
that I had never experienced.
"Well?" I asked her. I tried
to keep the impatience
out of my voice.
"What did the gods say?
Will I find love?"
She regarded me for a moment,
that smile still playing upon
her lips and dancing in her eyes.
Her smile deepened
and she nodded sagely.
"Amicus optima vitae possessio."
Her voice made the words
sound like music. I didn't understand.

"What does that mean?
Will I find love?"
She nodded again and uttered
the same words:
"Amicus optima vitae possessio."
I left her feeling distraught
and unsure of myself.
I was ready for love,
open to the possibility of it,
but the wise woman's words
meant nothing to me.
I found myself in front
of a bookstore filled with
old books. I went inside
and instantly found myself
calmed by the smell of
old parchment and ink.
There was a man behind the counter.
I asked him what the words meant,
what language they were in.
"Amicus optima vitae possessio…"
He mused. He went to a bookshelf
and pulled down a large volume
of Latin verse and terminology.
Flipping through pages
that sounded like the wind.
"It means 'A friend is
the greatest treasure of life.'"
I stood there for a moment,

processing what he'd told me.
"That doesn't make sense.
I asked the wise woman
whether or not
I would find love."
The man thought about
this for a moment. Then
he regarded me with eyes
that sparkled like the wise woman's.
"Well, do your friends love you?"
I didn't need to think of the answer.
"Yes. They're like my family of the heart."
He regarded me with something
like understanding.
"Then you are very fortunate.
If you are loved, by so many,
why do you seek more?"
I wondered at his question and
how exactly to answer it.
"Because I have so much love to give."
He smiled at me and it was like
the sun was shining on him.
"Then give it to your friends,
your family. You won't find love
if you are looking for it."
He touched my chest where my heart rested.
"Love finds you."
I thanked him and left the store,
my body lighter than it had been

when I entered.
"Amicus optima vitae possessio"
I whispered and felt very rich
indeed.

The Princess of Wands

* *For Carol, who is magical...*

When I saw her for the first time,
I thought my eyes were playing
tricks on me.
She was sitting against
a bright red wall, a soft light
playing off of her skin
and hair, as if she was
surrounded in light.
For a moment, I saw
a woman standing in front
of a dense forest.
She was holding a long staff
with light that shone
brighter than the sun
in one hand and in the other
a shield made of gold that
held the world.
Then I blinked my eyes
and the vision was gone.
As I grew to know her,
I realized that the light
she had didn't come
from a staff or shield.
It came from within her,

shining out in waves
that brightened the lives
of any she came close to.
She didn't need any wand
to make her magic.
She gave it freely to others,
those who were in pain
or suffering from hidden darkness
that the world couldn't see.
She took their pain
and left only light behind.
She doesn't need a wand
to make her magic.
She already is

The Possibility of Happenstance

The possibility thrilled me.
The thought that something was
waiting for me, right around
the corner. All I had to do
was wait for it.
I was impatient though
and couldn't wait.
I searched for it instead.
I looked everywhere
for this possibility, this
chance encounter that I
wanted with every
fibre of my being.
I looked around buildings
but only saw alley ways.
I looked into windows,
but only saw my reflection.
I looked in stores
and saw only masses
of people passing me by.
I would search the sky
for clues of my future,
I would read the fortunes that
came inside of cookies
to see when it would happen,
to see *if* it would happen.

I was looking so hard
that I almost missed it,
almost walked by it.
I was out looking at
life passing me by
when a stranger said to me:
"What are you looking for?"
I shook my head.
"I don't know."
I didn't know how
to put into words
the urgency I
was filled with.
The stranger, a woman
wearing a red dress
and black gloves
looked at me with a gaze
that saw everything.
"Well, until you
figure out what you're
searching for, isn't half
the fun in living?
Fate knows what it
has in store for you already.
The least you can do is
live your life until fate
delivers your due
and gets itself in order."
I shook my head.

"I don't understand you."
She threw up her hands
in exasperation.
"Why, you have to believe
in the possibility
of happenstance.
You have to engage with life,
truly live it.
Then that chance,
that possibility,
will show itself."
"How can I do that?"
I asked her. I was
mesmerized by her,
by the conviction
with which she spoke.
"By believing that
the impossible
isn't so impossible
after all."
She tipped her
head to me.
"I hope you find
what you're searching for.
But have fun
in the meantime, okay?"
She walked on
and I wondered
at the world

that had suddenly
grown brighter
around me.

Drawn Together

"What are you doing?"
Birth approached Life
at the easel.
She had a large canvas
propped upon it.
"Painting." Life replied.
"That looks horrible."
Death said, entering the room.
"You better throw it out."
the oldest Fate said.
"It's horrible."
"Oh, don't be such a downer."
Birth said. "After all,
I have my garden,
you have your singing,
let Life indulge in her creativity."
Death made a flippant
motion with her hand.
"Whatever." She said.
"What's it supposed to be anyways?"
Life looked at the canvas
with pride beaming off her face.
"Two men who
need to be drawn to each other."
"Men are pigs " Death said.
"Not all men," Birth replied.
"Some of them are nice."
19

"These two are wonderful." Life said.
"If they're wonderful,
why do they need help?" Death said,
scorn evident in her voice.
"Everyone needs a little help
where the heart is concerned." Life said.
"They just need a little nudge."
"Well, I think it's beautiful." Birth said.
"You haven't seen anything yet." Life replied.
She tapped her paint brush
on the canvass and the two men
walked towards each other
across the canvas
until they met in the middle
and enfolded each other
in an embrace.
Light began to shine
from the canvas
until even the
Three Fates were blinded
by its brilliance.

When You Became We

*For my Wonder Parents

I remember the day
you both said those
two words.
They seem so simple,
so easy to say
but they invoked
the most powerful
magic that is
still felt today.
Those words gave
one you a husband and
one of you a wife.
Those words declared
to the world
that you were meant
to be together,
that you were soul mates.
Your love has grown
from a small seed to
something that continues
to grow, as if it were
a tree that is
reaching for the sky.
The tree grows

21

larger and more full
with every year
that passes
and it all started
when You
became We
and the magic
of your love
started to grow.

A Gift of Joy

I was in a dark mood,
had been for days.
I walked down the
sidewalk and I passed by
a homeless woman.
I walked a little further
and then stopped.
Here was something
that I could do,
something that would
make me feel better.
I took out a handful
of change and walked
back to the homeless woman.
I put the money
into her battered
McDonald's cup,
thinking she was probably
going to spend it on
booze or drugs.
It didn't matter,
I had done my good deed.
I went into the bookstore
to give myself
a Zen moment and
the homeless woman
walked in behind me.

"Do you have that book you put on hold for me? I finally have enough! I got enough to get my book!"
The man behind
the counter went to get
her book and
I stood there, stunned.
I had assumed that
she'd be using the
money I'd given her
for something else
entirely. Never did it
occur to me that
she'd buy a book.
She stood there
holding the book
like a child and
the look on her face,
one of sheer joy
and absolute bliss,
was all I needed
to chase my dark mood
away.

Graveyard of Rings

We were going
through the jewellery
box, the bits
and pieces that
I held on
to. It was
a wooden box
with six drawers
made from unvarnished
wood. Each drawer
held something different.
The bottom one
held watches, the
middle two bracelets
and necklaces. The
forth and fifth
drawer held trinkets.
She pointed at
the sixth drawer.

                                    What's in that one?

It's my graveyard.
I said quietly.

                                    You're what?

I have the rings from every failed relationship in there.
    Why would you hold on to those? Why would you keep them?
To remember.

What exactly is it that you're remembering? How the relationships
ended?

I looked down
at the rings,
at the symbols
they had been
that had meant
so much to
me. One had
been in the
graveyard so long
that even the
stone had turned
from purple to
black. I looked
at the rings,
at the bonds
that they had
symbolized. Five rings
that had seemed
to mean so
much at the
time, however, their
light had dimmed,
the graveyard dark.
Do you think I should throw them out?

Well, it is your pack and purge party before the big move.

I took the
rings in my

hand and walked

to one of

the garbage bins.

I held out

my hand. I

thought of what

to say, to

commemorate the occasion.

Thanks for nothing.

I said, and

prepared to drop

them in the

garbage. She stopped

me. She shook

her head and

said very firmly.

> They weren't the right men for you. But they were what you
> needed then.

She looked at

me solemnly and

spoke these words:

Thank you for giving him what he needed then, but now he doesn't
need you anymore. He's letting you go.

She let go

of my hand

and I let

the rings slide

from my hand

and let go.

She closed the
bag and I
looked toward the
future.

We Are Who We Choose To Be

When I walked
into the club,
all I saw
was smoke. It
twisted in the
air around me
like wishes released
on a sigh,
taking form only
when it left
the person's lips.
The majority of
the smoke came
from two women
sitting at a
wooden table lit
by a candle
stuck inside of
a wine bottle.
The candle spluttered
and shook when
the women blew
out their smoke
wishes. One of
them turned to
me and waved
her hand through

the fog of
wishes not spoken.

Honey, what you doing all alone?
You look a little lost. Come and sit with us.
We won't bite unless you ask us to.

I nodded and
took a seat.
She had blond
hair, the other
had black and
both wore it
in tight ringlet's.

Look, Anna, he's blushing!
Oh, I haven't seen a man sensible enough to blush in years.
Don't be shy honey. Here, have a glass of spirits.
If it's called spirits, it must be good for the spirit, right?

I nodded again
and took the
glass that was
offered to me.
The liquid inside
was clear and
I wondered what
it was. I took
a sip and
my throat started
burning immediately. I
started to cough
and shake. The

blond haired one
patted my hand.

Oh sugar, this your first time
with a drink? Here, try a cigarette
instead. It's an easier vice.

I took one
and she leaned
forward to light
it for me.
In the brilliance
of the flame
I saw what
I didn't before.
Are you a man?
I asked, not
thinking before I
spoke. She looked
at me with
a smile on
her round face.

Oh honey, don't you wish.
I may have a dick, but I'm
all woman. Don't you forget it!
Anna, don't scare the poor boy, he doesn't
know where he is and he doesn't need
you frightening him.
Well, Gaia, the boy has to know.
He has to understand. He has
to comprehend why we are

31

the way we are.

I took another
drag off of
the cigarette and
let my wishes
join the others
in the air.

What do I have to understand?

> *Well sugar, it's like this. We may have*
> *been born as men, but we're woman,*
> *through and through. It's as simple*
> *as that.*

I shook my
head and the
room wavered. I
took another sip
of spirit juice,
another drag of
wishes. The black
haired one, Gaia,
smiled at me.

> *Anna forgets that it's not so simple.*
> *It takes people a long time to learn*
> *this, but I'm going to tell you for free.*
> *This is important. You may not speak easy,*
> *but you listen well. So are you listening?*

I nodded and took
more wishes into
my lungs. I

32

imagined it filling
me with light.

What you have to remember
is this: we are who we choose to be.
You want to be a writer?
Be a writer. You want to be fabulous,
be fabulous. You got it?

I nodded, but
something nagged at
me. I took
another drag off
my wish stick.

It can't be that simple. You can't just choose to be who you
want to be.

Anna laughed and
patted my hand
again. She cackled
like she'd never
heard anything funnier.

Of course it is honey! You are
the only one standing in your own
way. Your whole life is out there,
waiting to be lived. So give yourself
a kick in the ass to get out of your
own way and live it. Now
make a wish.

I stared at
them, their kind
faces, the make-up

33

starting to slide
off their skin
from the heat
in the bar.
It was their
light I saw,
shining from within.
I took another
drag off my
cigarette and let
the smoke flow
from my mouth
to join the
cloud that hung
above us. My
wish was made.
I already knew
who I would
choose to be.
I just had
to get out
of my way
and live the
dream worth living.

What The Empress Had To Say

I kept seeing the same woman
everywhere I went. She would
leave a trail of cards behind her
as if they were flower petals.
I would approach her, hoping
that she would slow down and
I would be able to catch up
to her, but she always moved
just out of my reach. I tried
to collect the cards, but they
would start to melt,
turning to water before I could
begin to gather them.
I was able to see colours and shapes
before they faded away
but nothing more.
Another woman saw me
trying to gather the cards.
She carried a staff that
shone with a light all its own.
"The Empress is trying to
tell you something."
I noticed that this woman
was wearing a golden
helmet with two horns that
twisted into the sky. When I
looked again, the horns were gone.

"What's that?" I said. "What
Is she trying to tell me?"
The woman with the horns
shrugged. "Only you can know.
However, I can give you a piece
of advice. If you're willing to listen."
It was my turn to shrug. "Okay.
I'm listening." I stood there,
the puddles left by the cards
forming a line of water along
the pavement. The water
looked like jewels catching the sun.
"Don't look for what you think
your heart wants. That will lead
to disappointment. Instead,
listen to your heart. It will tell
you what it needs."
"When?" I said. I tried to keep
the frustration out of my voice.
"When you're willing to listen."
She said. She bowed her head to me,
and followed the path that
the Empress had taken, using
the water to guide her.
I noticed that she had a
golden disk strapped to her back.
As she moved away from me,
I blinked again and the horns returned.
I watched her until the shadows claimed her.

I returned home to find a small package
on my front stoop surrounded
by water. I picked it up and
unwrapped it, revealing a deck of cards.
I knew this was from the Empress.
These were the cards that had
trailed behind her like flower petals.
I took the cards inside and
as I flipped through them,
I listened to what the Empress
had to say.

In Time

I was in a shop that sold time.
The shop was filled with tick-tocking
and soft plinks as grains of sand
hit against glass. All kinds of watches
were on display. As I looked around
the shop, I noticed the people within.
They were all men I had been with,
men that I had loved, at one time
or another. They all turned towards me.
Each came closer, holding out
a watch for me. The first
held out a watch made from
glass, it's strap covered
in shards that would only
draw blood from me.
"You would look wonderful wearing this."
I backed away from him.
"No, I don't want that."
The next man held out a watch
with a strap made from barbed wire.
"You should wear this one."
I pushed it away. "I can't wear that."
Then one held out a woman's watch,
covered in pearls and rubies.
"This one would look great on you."
"No." I said. "It wouldn't."
The next man held out a watch made from

steel and it looked heavy and cold.
"This is your watch." He said.
I shook my head again.
"No, it's not." I turned and looked
at the room of men I had
loved and shook my head.
"None of you knew me at all." I said.
"I choose none of the watches."
I looked at each of the men in the eye,
met each of their stares with my own.
"I tell my own time now."
When I left the shop,
It was without a watch but with
all the time in the world.

Joy and Light

* For Rachael for she is fabulous.

You are light and brightness
personified. You are joy
and comfort made real.
You are strength and
support given form.
As you take another
step along your path,
we are all celebrating
with you, as our lives
are made better
for knowing you.

<u>Magic and Mannequins</u>

I passed by the store window
and for a moment thought
the mannequins were real people.
I wondered why they were
stuck behind the glass.
Then it occurred to me
what they were, that
they weren't real,
no matter how lifelike
they looked. I was about to
keep walking when one of
the mannequins winked at me.
I stared, thinking I had
imagined it. She was pretty,
with a short blond bob,
her eyes covered with
blue eye shadow that
made her grey eyes sparkle.
She winked at me again
and one of her fingers
wiggled at me, telling me
to come closer. Swallowing
my fear, I went into the store.
It smelled of honeysuckle
and roses. A kindly woman
stood behind the counter.
How may I help you sir?

Her voice was like music

and had a lilt to it that

I couldn't recognize.

I'm sorry, this is going to sound nuts, but-

One of the ladies winked at you, didn't they?

She said this with a smile,

as if it were an everyday occurrence.

How did you know?

Oh, they wink at people who need the most assistance.

What kind of assistance?

Oh, all kinds of things. Lost keys, lost hearts, lost dreams. Which
one was it that winked at you?

I turned and looked at

the mannequins and pointed

at the one with the blonde bob.

It was her.

Oh, Estelle! She helps those seeking love! She's delightful. If she's
brought you in here, it won't take long now. She's very good.

What do you mean?

Watch.

A man was walking by the store

and stopped just as I had. He looked

at the blonde haired mannequin, Estelle,

and I watched as she crooked a finger at him.

He was tall with sandy coloured hair

and soft blue eyes. I saw him blink

in surprise and then look at the store.

How does she know he's someone I'll fall in love with? Are the
mannequins alive?

The woman laughed and it was a sound
that reminded me of the tinkling of bells.
If I told you, you wouldn't believe me.
Try me.
Magic.
I laughed. **Magic? Really?**
She smiled. *There are all kinds of magic. You just have to be open
enough to receive them.*
The bell above the door jangled
as the man entered the store.
When he looked at me, a spark
passed between us. It zapped
through the air and heat ran
along my body.

See? She said.
Magic.

Sirens, Smoke and Scarves

I was walking
along the sidewalk.
There was a
sound of sirens
in the air
and the third
fire truck I
had seen z   o   o   m   e   d
by me. A
woman I didn't
know stopped in
front of me.

What do you think is going on?
I had no idea.

That's the sixth one I've seen. I saw three more earlier.
There must be something terrible happening.
We watched as
even more of
them arrived, their
lights flashing in
the air like
clouds filled with
lightning. The woman
pointed to one
of the bright
red engines. It
looked like a

slash of blood
on the pavement.

    That must be the fire marshal. What do you think he's doing with
                                 that canister?

                I don't-

My words were
cut off when
the earth shook
around us and
the air filled
with screaming. People
started to fall
from far up,
hitting the ground
as if they
were embracing it.
One girl landed
by my feet,
hitting the ground
with a sickening
splat. The woman
beside me began
crying. The girl
was still alive,
breathing with a
wet hollow sound.

                            Where's the smoke?

One boy cried.

                            Where's the fucking fire?

45

I kneeled down
beside the girl
and held her.
I wanted her
last moment to
be one of
kindness. She turned
her eyes towards
mine and they
were glassy with
pain. She reached
out one hand
to my scarf,
smearing it's red
and gold colours
with blood She
spoke so softly.

Harry Potter?

She said. I
could only nod.

I like your scarf.

She said. Then
she closed her
eyes as the world
came apart around
all of us
and the air
began to fill
with fog like

46

smoke until I
could no longer
see the girl.
She held on
to my scarf
though, and refused
to let go.

Keep Walking and Be Fabulous

I could hear
them as they
walked up the
sidewalk. One man
was wearing a
bright red shirt
that said "My
other car is
a Delorean" and
the other wore
a backwards baseball
cap with the
words "Yo Bitches"
stitched in black.
You SO cannot tell who's gay. What do you know about gay
people?
The one in
the hat said,
his voice full
of derision and
disdain. His friend
in the Delorean
t-shirt punched him
in the arm.
I can SO tell who's gay Like that guy there? He's gay. There's a
girl on his t-shirt and no self respecting straight guy would wear
that.

Hermione from the
Harry Potter series
was on my shirt.
That didn't matter
though. You can't
tell what sexuality
someone is from
what they're wearing.
As they came
closer, Delorean stepped
in my path.
Yo, question for you. Are you gay?
I wondered how
to respond to
him. Educate or
mock him? I
decided on mockery.
I AM very happy, thank you for asking.
No, what I meant was-
I know what you meant. And what does that matter?
Delorean pointed to
Yo Bitches and
gave me a
smile that was
meant to put
me at ease.
My friend here and I are trying to settle an argument.
I decide to
play dumb. It's

worked well before.

What argument is that?

Whether you can tell if someone is gay by what they're wearing.

I look them

both up and

down. I smile.

Don't worry. No one can tell, just keep walking and be fabulous.

Their stunned looks

are joined by

my laughter as

I walk away.

A Pocket Full of Light

How are you sir?
I turned around
and saw the
man who had
been working the
table in front
of me. The
table was covered
in all sorts
of rings and
things that glittered.
I'm fine, thank you.
And how is your pocket?
My pocket?
I reached into
it and pulled
out some Kleenex
and a pack
of gum. I
showed them to
him, unsure of
what this was
about. A woman
behind him said:
Where did you put the silver ring?
It's right there on the table.
I didn't like

51

where this was
going. Being accused
of theft amongst
a crowd of
people, all of
them looking at
me. I pointed:
It's right there, in the display tray.
**I saw you put something into your pocket. Make him empty
the other one.**
The woman was
scowling, trying to
figure out what
I had done
when I had
done nothing wrong.
Would you mind sir? Empty the other pocket please.
I nodded, not
wanting to anger
either of them.
I unzipped my
pocket and the
store became brighter
as if lit
by the sun.
<u>What is that?</u>
Another woman said
this, and she
leaned down to

look in my
coat pocket. I
saw more light
as she opened
it further. She
let out a
small, soft cry.
When she stood,
she was crying
but a smile
was on her
face, making her
ten years younger.
*I just saw myself dancing with my husband. That was fifty years
ago and he's ten years gone. It was the happiest moment of my life.
Thank you.*
She touched my
arm and another
person moved forward,
this time a
man. He was
old and walked
with a cane.
Mind if I have a look?
He bent down
and looked inside
my pocket. The
brilliance of light
increased around us.

He let the
pocket close and
stood back up.
He was smiling
from ear to
ear, and his
smile radiated a
glow that matched
his eyes. He
shook my hand.

Thank you, sir! Thank you! I saw the day I met my husband. We've been together for thirty years but only got married a few years ago. God, he looked so good back then. Still does.

He gave me
his cane with
a roguish wink.

I won't be needing this anymore.

People began to
gather closer to
me, all of
them looking at
my pocket with
intense curiosity. The
woman who had
accused me stared
with something like
hunger. The man
who ran the
store came closer.

Can you empty your pocket sir? I'd like to see what's in there for myself.

I nodded, not
sure of what
else to say.

Don't do it! It's a trick! He's working magic!

She licked her
lips as she
said this, hungry
even for something
she didn't understand.
I reached into
my pocket and
felt something there,
a sphere shaped
object. Slowly I
pulled it out
of my pocket
The brightness was
instantaneous and as
I held onto
the sphere, the
light grew even
brighter still. I
wondered if the
light was coming
from the sphere
or from me.
As more people

cried out, each
seeing the moment
in their lives
that had made
them the happiest,
I could resist
no longer. I
looked directly into
the light and
saw a man's
face. I wondered
who he could
be, who he
was. I had
never seen him
before. The light
began to dim
slowly as if
receding back into
the sphere. When
it was dark
again, I looked
up and saw
the man I
had seen in
the light across
the room, looking
right at me.
As he walked

towards me, I
could feel the
sphere grow warm.
As he drew
closer to me,
brightness bloomed once
more. Then he
was right in
front of me
and took my
free hand in his.
The brilliance grew
brighter still until
we were both
bathed in light.

Beautiful Leaves

* For Michael who is a wish granted.

The first time I saw you,
I heard the rustle of leaves.
Looking down at your feet,
I expected to see them there,
covering the floor,
but it was bare.
The first time you took my hand,
I heard the whisper of leaves
and a breeze rose up
around us. It was filled
not with leaves, but
with fractures of light
filling the air like dreams
given physical form.
The first time we kissed,
I once again heard
the crinkle of leaves.
Opening my eyes,
I saw they surrounded us,
fluttering through the air,
as if we were at the centre
of a whirlwind.
When you took your lips
away from mine,
the beautiful leaves

gave a happy sigh,
as if in content and
flew into the wind
away from us.
As they flew up
towards the sky,
so did my heart,
swelling full of wind
infused with wishes
made reality. Letting out
a happy sigh of my own,
I leaned in to kiss you again
and heard only
the sound of wind
and wishes fulfilled.

Beautiful As You Are

* For Dawn, who is Beauty personified.

She was sitting
at her vanity
mirror when I
walked into her
bed chamber. She
stared at herself
in the mirror,
frowning. A sad
look made
her face seem
longer than it
was. She saw
me come into
the room and
turned to me.
He eyes were
bloodshot and lost.

What's wrong? What has you so upset?

There was no
build up to
her sadness or
her anguish. I
wanted to take
her pain away.

Look at me! Look at what I've become! I used to be beautiful!

60

She reached out
a hand to
touch the mirror.
It began to
shimmer and the
surface rippled like
water. As I
watched, the mirror's
reflection changed. Now
it was as
if we were
looking at a
large photo. Her
younger self stared
back at us.

I used to be beautiful! Look at me then! I had everything! High
cheek bones,
plump lips, tits that didn't sag.

As I watched,
her skin began
to glow along
the lines of
her wrinkles, as
if her younger
self was shining
through, trying to
get out again.
I went to
her and put

a hand on her
shoulder. She looked
up at me.

You are beautiful.

I said. She
made a derisive
noise in the
back of her
throat and rolled
her eyes. Her
skin still glowed.

You are. You bring joy to many and just by knowing you,
their lives are made more beautiful.
Would you want to be a carbon copy
of what you used to be?

The glow from
her skin began
to dim. It
was softer now
and growing duller
by the moment.

You really think so? You really, truly think so?

You're beautiful as you are.

I told her.
The mirror
behind us began
to shimmer once
more and when
the ripples stopped,

another picture had
taken its place.
Now, there was
a photo of
her as she
was. She looked
closely at herself.
The smile she
wore was brilliant
like the sun.
She touched the
glass and at
her touch, the
picture inside the
mirror faded. As
it did, the
glow from her
skin increased until
she was bathed
in light. She
turned back to
me and took
my hand in
hers. There were
tears sliding down
her cheeks, her
lips curved in
a brilliant smile.

I'm beautiful as I am.

She said. The
light from her
grew brighter still.
She let out
a laugh that
was like music.

I'm beautiful as I am.

A Torrent of Black Pearls

I couldn't keep
all of myself
inside of me.
There was too
much of it,
too much shadow
and darkness, grief
and self-doubt and
it consumed me,
filling me with
a tar-like substance
that would slip
through my skin,
staining my clothes.
A smell came
from my clothes
and there was
a look about me
of quiet desperation.
I could barely
walk at that point
and was like
the third part
of the Sphinxes
riddle. I was
cold even in
the glorious heat

of the sun.
I was lost
within myself no
longer able to
hold myself together.
I was breaking
like glass streaked
with smoke. I
sat in the sun,
its fierce brightness
shining down on
me and I felt
nothing. I closed
my eyes and
drifted on a
dark turbulent sea
that threw its waves
against the inside
of me. Tears
slipped out of
my eyes like
black pearls. They
landed in my
lap and I
tried to catch
them. It was
then that she
spoke to me:

"Now why would you want to hold on to that shit for?"

I opened my
eyes and saw
a woman sitting
beside me. She
had kind eyes,
deep golden brown.
The sun shone
around her like
a halo. She
was motioning
at the pearls
of my despair.

"They are all I have left."

I told her.
The words were
thick coming out
of my mouth.

"They are all I know now."

She gave me a
kind look of
such understanding, of
knowing that more
black pearls began
to slide, slide
down my cheeks.

**"You can't heal with all of that inside you if you don't let all of
that go, how do you expect to fill the empty spaces with
something else?"**

I looked at

67

her and couldn't
tell what age
she was. She
could be twenty
or thirty-five. She
reached out and
took my hands
in hers. The
pearls in my
palms fell to
the ground. Her
hands were as
warm as the sun.
I shook my head,
uttering words that
I had kept close,
inside the shadows.

"I don't know what to do now. I'm so afraid all the time. I can't live like this. I've been thinking of ending it, just calling it quits. Of giving up."

She gave me
another look of
understanding, as if
she had been
exactly where I
was before, as
if she knew.
She nodded and
didn't have to say

anything but
then she did,
in the softest,
kindest of voices.

"You are not a quitter. It's not in you. Let the darkness go. It will be okay."

She squeezed my
hand and I knew
that it would
be. I nodded
and even that
small movement of
agreement was like
a knife blade
severing that which
had been holding
me back. The broken
shadows began to
fall away from
me, a slow
trickle of pearls
that *plunked* and
plinked and *clicked*
on the grass
and the bench.
The trickle soon
increased, real tears,
stained black by
the smoke shadows

inside of me
flowing from my
eyes. I tried
to cover my
eyes to stem
the flow of
the tears. She
pulled my hands
back down into
my lap. I
looked at her.

"When the darkness is gone, what do I fill the emptiness with?
I've lived with these shadows for so long. I don't know who I am
anymore."

She interlaced her
fingers in mine
and the heat
from her hands
increased, filling me
with such warmth.

"You can fill the emptiness with new things. Let the past go.
Only then can you discover who you are meant to be."

I nodded again,
the motion another
swipe at the
web of smoke
and shadow that
I wore around
myself. The tears

came then, a
flood of black
tears that soaked
my shirt, my
clothes, the grass.
They stopped for
a moment, as
if taking a
breath or pause.
Then more tears
came, but they
were not filled
with smoke. These
were real tears,
clear and pure.
They became
a torrent that
lifted the black
pearls and slid
them along through
the grass, away
from me. Once
the last black
pearl vanished, the
tears stopped, I
sat there, wet
with spent emotion
and looked at
the woman again.

She had not
let go, had
held my hands
the entire time.

"Do you feel better?"

She asked me.

"Yes."

I said. I
felt empty but
I didn't feel
heavy anymore. I
wasn't weighed down
by my past.
I had let
it all go.

"Good,"

She said, her
voice kind, soft.

"Now the healing can begin."

"What will happen?"

"You'll let your true self shine. That's all you have to do."

The sun framing
her head like
a halo grew
brighter and I
had to look
away, close my
eyes. When the
sun dimmed, I

looked back. The
woman was gone,
but I still
felt her hands
grasping mine and
I realized I
no longer felt
alone.

The Princess of Cups

* *For Jayne, who is stronger than she knows*

When I first saw her,
tears were sliding down
her cheeks. Though they
were tears of grief,
they shone on her face
like dew drops made
from her sadness.
As I watched the tears
leave her eyes, they began
to shape a necklace made
of jewels that shone as
bright as stars. They
reflected the light within her
that shone so brightly.
As I've come to know her,
she has filled my life
with her light and her
joy. She has
astounded me with
her kindness, her
tenderness, her
willingness to love.
It's as if she stands
at the centre of an
island, surrounded

by the seas over
which she travelled.
She ignores the castle,
tall and dark and instead
chooses to stand on the sand
so that the water from
the waves can touch her skin.
As I've come to know more,
I am astounded and inspired
by her strength, her will
and her wisdom.
Over time, the
necklace of stars
has become a crown,
sitting proudly on her head,
letting her light shine out
for all to see.
She has left the island
to embrace life and all
that it has to offer.

Life is a Journey

Excuse me?
I looked up.
It was a
man that I
recognized, but I
didn't know from
where. It must
have shown on
my face. I've
never been good
at hiding things
within my skin.
You probably don't remember me. I saw you walking down the
sidewalk with your cane during the summer. I said we were both
Children of the Sphinx.
As soon as
he said that,
I did remember.
The riddle of
the Sphinx ran
through my head:
What walks on four legs in the morning, two legs in the
afternoon, three legs in the evening?
I said. His
eyes widened and
he smiled at
me, clapping a

hand to my
arm in joy.
You do remember! And look at you now! Walking without your
third leg! How did you do that?
I thought about
how to answer
him, how to
encompass everything I'd
been through to
get where I
am. In the
end, I just
shrugged my shoulders.
He put his
hand on my
arm again and
left it there.
It's okay, you don't need to say anything. Life doesn't often work
out the way we think it will. Life doesn't go as we plan it or dream
it when we're young.
I nodded. He
had summed up
everything I had
been thinking. I
looked at him,
really took him
in, his kind
eyes, warm smile
and his right

hand, holding a
long wooden cane.

No, it doesn't. Mine certainly hasn't.

He looked at
me, taking me
in this time.
He nodded his
head, looked at
me with wise
and open eyes.

*Can I ask you something? You have the look of someone who's
been on a journey. You have, haven't you?*

I nodded again,
unable to say
anything. I was
normally not at
a loss for
words, but this
man's ability to
see right into
me silenced them.

*Then I want you to do something for me. Every time you start to
slide back, I want you to take a stop on the path you're on and look
back at how far you've come. Will you do that.*

I said softly.

Yes, I will.

Good.

He said, giving
me a smile.

Just remember, You're life may have not gone as planned, but
that's okay. It's all a journey. All of it.
He hugged me
then with one
arm, the other
one still down,
holding the cane.
I hugged him
back with both
arms, trying to
communicate everything that
I hadn't said.
You take care of yourself now. Okay?
He walked away
down the sidewalk
With the sun
shining behind him,
his shadow looked
as if he
didn't have a
cane in his
grasp and seemed
to stretch until
it was as
tall as the
Sphinx.

The Voice of Inspiration

* For my Wonder Mum, who said the words that shone through the water.

You should only write if you're inspired.
Her voice was
a balm to
me. She was
my touchstone, my
rock. I thought
of what she
said, of her
wisdom. I thought
of the endless
nights I had
spent trying to
see through the
fog that engulfed
me, of the
frustration of looking
at a blank
screen. It mocked
me like an
unblinking eye. I
tried to give
words to what
I was feeling.
I'm a writer. I can't be a writer if I don't write.

Her voice became
softer. It was
the voice I
always called to
mind when I
imagined her speaking
to me. Hearing
it was no
different. It was
instantly, incredibly comforting:
You will always be a writer, whether or not you're writing. It's in
you, it's what you do. It's who you are. Let the words come on
their own. They will come when they are ready.
I carried her
words home with
me, as if
they had a
physical form. When
I got home,
I was weighed
down. I put
my hands in
my pockets and
found they were
full of stones.
Each stone had
a word painted
on one side
in metallic paint

that looked like
water. I let
the stones fall
where they would
onto the floor.
Everywhere a stone
fell, water began
to spread from
beneath it, until
my floor was
covered in water
as deep as
an ocean. Looking
at all the
words shining from
underneath the waves.
Now that I
was no longer
weighed down by
them, it was
time to swim
into the water
and see what
the words had
to say to
me.

The Forever Forest

Before we entered
the forest, you
took my hand.
A shiver of
warmth spread through
me and I
heard a sound
on the wind
that was made
from a thousand
branches clattering together.
I looked at
the dark forest
and felt a
moment of trepidation.
You squeezed my
hand and pulled
me even closer.
Don't be afraid. I'm with you.
I shook my
head, my voice
thick in my
throat. Finally, I
pushed it out.
I've already been here. This was part of my journey. I know
this forest well.
You looked at

me with such
kindness, such warmth.
Now you don't have to go through the forest alone. I'm beside you.
You started forward
and I followed.
As we approached
the first set
of trees, they
started to change.
The bark started
to shift, growing
more whole, their
pockmarks and cracks
repairing themselves, the
branches growing straighter,
reaching for the
sky. I watched
as leaves began
to bloom on
the branches, the
green bright against
the bark. You
pointed deeper into
the forest and
I saw that
all the trees
were healing, becoming
whole again, leaves
re-growing. I felt

a light growing
inside of me,
pulsing through me,
living inside of
me. I looked
at you and
even *you* seemed
brighter to me.

What did you do to me?

You did this yourself. You've grown anew, just like the trees.

You motioned to
the forest and
smiled at me.

Come on, let's go deeper along the path, as far as we can go.

I've already been through here.

This is the same forest, true, but now you've found a way forward.

Now we can go forward together.

You kissed me
then and I
heard the forest
make a sound
that was like
music. I listened
as a breeze ruffled
all the leaves
at once. It
was as if they
were voicing
their approval. I

entered deeper into
the forest, my
hand in yours,
looking around at
all the trees.
They had been
dark, empty husks
but were now
full of life.
I knew exactly
how they felt.
I squeezed your
hand tighter and
took comfort from
you, from your
touch, from the
love that flowed
from you to
me and back
again. I took
in all of
you and knew
that anything was
possible. There was
nothing to fear
in the trees.
There was only
the promise of
forever. I breathed

you in and
stepped with you,
further into the
forest.

Doubt Dragons and the Lioness

* For Heather, with my thanks and gratitude. You're awesome.

I was moved to go in.
Something about the store
called to me. It was as if
there was a heady kind of
music playing from within.
It sounded like flute music,
but soulful and filled with
understanding. When I went in,
a set of chimes rang above
my head. I was struck by
how warm and inviting
the store was, how alive
I felt within the confines
of its walls. I knew that
nothing could hurt me here.
Standing behind the counter
was the source of the light
that thrived around me.
She had a brilliant smile
and black hair that framed
her face in a riot of curls.
I blinked and, for a second,
thought I saw a being in front
of me like a lioness, staring
into me with bright yellow

eyes that saw everything.
I blinked and she was
the woman again. She
came towards me with
her hands held out.
"Hey stranger!"
I didn't know how to
respond to her.
"Hello. Have we met before?"
She gave me a
wise look and I could
swear that her eyes
changed from blue to yellow
and back again.
"Oh, we've all met before. You look like a man in need."
"In need of what?"
*"We're all in need of something. I sense that you need help with
doubt."*
My breath was taken from me.
"How could you know that?"
She gave me another wise look.
*"We're all filled with doubt, some more than others. Some are
easy to slay, others take a little bit more persuasion."*
I found myself nodding, knowing
that she knew what lived inside
of me, despite my best intentions.
"How do I do that? How do I slay them?"
Her eyes became yellow again
for a moment and I saw the

ears of a lioness poking through
her curly black hair. Then
she was herself again. I
wondered which face was
truly hers, the lady or the lioness,
or if they were one and the same?

"Doubts are like Dragons. You can't slay them with swords or knives though. You can only slay them with your will. It has to be strong."

"It is strong. It is."
I knew this. I knew this
with all of my heart.

"Then you must take that strength and use it. Envision your life, exactly as it should be. Do this every single day. Feel it, smell it, hear it."

"Then the doubt dragons will leave?"

"Only if you envision them gone. Envision your life exactly as you want it. The Doubt Dragons will lose interest and fly away; but you have to let them go."

I was silent for a moment,
knowing that she spoke
only the truth. Already
I felt a surge of warmth
inside me, knowing that
I was going to be okay.

"Thank you."
She laughed and the
sound was like the wind chimes
that had been above the

door of the Lioness' shop.

"Oh, don't thank me. You've got to do all the work. I just put you on the right path."

"Can I come and see you again?"
She took my hand then and
I felt her warmth. It was
like she embodied the sun.

"Come and see me anytime. I'll be here."

As I left the store, the wind chimes
sang again. Their music
made me think of angels
getting their wings. I
wondered if I had just
been given my own.

<u>The Power of Forgetting</u>

I was blinded
by the sun
and didn't see
him until he
was walking next
to me. He smiled
and I was
struck by how
insincere it was.
Long time no see. How have you been?
I tried to
place him. I
had no idea
who he was
but he seemed
to know me.
Fine thanks. How about you?
He kept pace
with me. I
looked at his
face and tried
to place him,
to find a
name, tried to
find something familiar
in his facial
features. There was

nothing, no spark
of recognition. I
didn't know him.
Life is good. My grandparents just got back from Paris. They
always liked you.
Oh, that's nice.
I still had
no idea who
he was, how
I had known
him. He smiled
falsely at me.
How's your husband?
I don't have a husband. I have a boyfriend and he's lovely.
Oh, that's nice.
He echoed my
words back at
me and the
entire conversation felt
all odd and
out of place.
I pointed across
the street with
a wave of
my hand. I
shrugged at him.
I'm going that way. Sorry.
That's okay, I'm going this way. It was nice seeing you again.
Yeah, nice to see you.

The words weren't
true, but they
felt more polite
than telling him
I didn't know
who he was.
I walked on,
away from him
and his weird,
fake smile. It
was only hours
later that I
remembered who he
was and what
he had done
to me. I
had assumed that
I would always
remember him, that
I would never
forget him and
his cruelty. I
had carried those
memories with me
for a long
time. Too long.
I had forgotten
him, had forgotten
the shape of his

face, the contours
of his brow.
His face was
erased from my
memory and consciousness.
As I realized
that I had
forgotten who he
was, I also
let go of
who he had
been. I went
back out into
the sunshine and
felt a lot
brighter in body
mind and spirit.
I had let
a piece of
my past go
and looked
forward to what
the future would
bring.

Focusing the Light

Once when I
was younger my
consciousness was broad
and far reaching.
It only saw
the bigger picture
and didn't take
the time to
think about the
smaller joys that
life offered. It
was only concerned
with what I
would become rather
than what I
already was. I
was always on
the go, always
moving and never
still. It took
an event that
shook me to
the core, that
reshaped my body
and my soul
to draw my
vision into focus.

It narrowed the
wide beam of
light that flowed
from me, sharpened
it, gave it
more heat. Now
all I see
and all I
know is what
I am truly
capable of. My
consciousness is still
big, my desires
and dreams still
larger than life,
but they have
been given a
new purpose. I
am capable of
anything I set
my mind to
and all of
my dreams
are possible.

Wishful Thinking

I wished for
what I thought
to be impossible.
I had been
mistreated and scorned
by love, so
instead, wished for
what I thought
was only a
flight of fancy.
I went out
into the garden,
the moonlight shining
on all of
the flowers, their
blooms moving gently
in the wind.
I worked methodically,
picking blooms from
all kinds of
flowers. There were
petals from all
sorts of flowers,
pieces of a
love I didn't
think actually existed:
Freesia,

Daisies
Arbutus
Balsam
Forget Me Not
Globe Amaranth
Rose
Gathering some petals
from each flower,
I took them
back inside.
I ground all
the petals up
into a fine
powder, their colours
mingling with each
other until they
looked like nothing
but multi-coloured sand.
Going to the
front door, I
opened it to
find a strong
breeze had risen
up. I held out
the bowl of
powdered flower petals
and offered it
to the wind.
There were no

words I could
say, for how
did I put
into words that
which I thought
an impossible kind
of love, one
that I was
not destined for?
The wind took
the powder up
into its embrace
and carried it
away. I thought
that was it,
I was done.
Going back inside,
I let sleep
claim me and
was woken hours
later by a
knock at the
door. I sat
up, clutched the
blanket to my
chin. Slowly, I
stood up, my
feet shaky, unsure.
I made my

way to the
door and opened
it. The sunlight
shone around you
momentarily, like a
halo, as if
you were made
of the sun.

"Hello."
You said. Your
voice was deep
and melodious. Something
inside of me
stirred at the
sound of it.

"What is that gorgeous scent? What is it?"
"It's nothing, merely a wish."
I tried to
keep my voice
nonchalant, not daring
to hope but
believing in hope
all the same.

"I've been dreaming of that scent. It's what led me to you."
When you came
closer to me
and wrapped your
arms around me,
a wind began

to rise up
around us. When
you put your
lips to mine,
the wind began
to shine, as
if all the
flower petals, the
pieces of them,
were reflective and
shone even brighter.
"I wished for you."
You said. I
looked deep into
your eyes and
saw myself there.
"I guess wishes do come true."
I replied and
kissed you again,
the sunlight growing
brighter, reflected off
of the power
of a wish.

Three of Me

I was trying

to explain my

body to someone

else. She listened

closely, her face

showing openness, concern.

I often feel as if there are three of me in one body.

She cocked her

head to one

side, giving me

a confused look.

What do you mean?

I thought of

how to answer

her, how best

to phrase it.

**Well, the Cerebral Palsy is strongest on the right and the
Multiple Sclerosis is strongest on the left.**

Don't they affect your whole body?

Yes, but they've each taken sides, leaving me in the centre.

Sounds like quite the game of tug and war.

It is.

I paused for

a beat before

I told her.

I've named them.

Them? Them who?

Well, I'm a writer. I conquer fears by giving the fear a name. So I've given the CP and MS names.

Like characters in your books?

Exactly like that.

Her face softened

and she smiled

What are their names?

Well, I've named the Cerebral Palsy Cybil Paulesn and I've named the Multiple Sclerosis Max Shadow.

There was a

moment where I

wasn't sure what

she was going

to say. Then

her smile split

to let out

a delighted laugh.

I'm sorry! I've just never heard of someone naming their disabilities before.

She wiped away

tears from her

eyes which were

sparkling and full

of simple amusement.

I let out

a chuckle of

my own and

was immediately lighter.

If they're going to be with me for the rest of my life, I have to get to know them well.
I said. She
gave me another
one of her
warm smiles and
laid a hand
on my shoulder.
You already do. They're part of you and you know yourself now.
I pondered what
she said and
felt Cybil and
Max loosening their
hold a little,
just for a
moment, as if
breathing a sigh
of intimate understanding.

The Queen of Wands

* For Alexandra, who is a true Queen of Wands.

When I think
of her, I
picture her inside
a fencing arena.
She is holding
an épée. As
she lunges and
parries with her
opponent, she moves
with sure grace
and precision. All
of her movements
are filled with
passion and she
fights with honour,
with intent, all
of her steps
are like poetry
in motion. However,
when she lunges
closer for the
final blow, something
changes. A fire
begins to flow

from the tip
of her épée
and swims down
her arm, until
the flame and
fire surrounds her.
I see her
thus for only
a moment, her
sword transformed into
a wand held
high above her,
a fierce beautiful
light shining from
her eyes, before
she makes her
final lunge. When
her wand hits
the other opponent,
a shower of sparks
fills the air
around her.
She is passion,
strength and magic
given living form.
When she turns
to me, a
brilliant smile on
her face, she is

herself again but
leaves a trail
of sparks behind
her.

<u>Letting the Anchors Fly</u>

I was at
the water again.
The waves lapped
at the shoreline
and I wondered
how easy it
would be to
walk into the
water with all
that held me
down. I was
looking so hard
at the waves
that I didn't
hear her approach.
You look like Scrooge's ghost.
She said. Her
voice was deep,
her face lined.
She looked older
than time itself.
I'm sorry?
Scrooge's ghost. Marley! That's it. He had chains, but you got ghosts.
What are you talking about?
You don't see them, but they're there all the same. Can't you feel them?

I just have these.
I held out
my arm. It
was tattooed with
seven different anchors,
etched into my
skin with ink.
She laughed long
and hard, as
if she had
never seen anything
quite so funny.
That explains why they're around you, following you like lost puppies. What are they for?
I bristled at
her laughter and
drew myself up.
They remind me not to forget. They remind me of what happened.
Of where I came from.
She looked at
me, gave me
a stern look
that was somehow
kind and saw
into me, into
the very heart
of me. I
looked back at
her, trying to

communicate what I

was feeling inside.

She nodded, as

if she understood.

At that nod,

I heard the

jingle jangle of

chains rattling around

both of us.

Honey, we all have shit that people have done, that people have said. Even if we've dealt with that shit, it can still weigh us down, even if no one else can see it. You've got to let the anchors go.

Unbeknownst to me,

tears started to

fall from my

eyes and I

did nothing to

stop their flow.

I don't know how.

I said. My

voice wobbled and

was approaching a

loud pitched wail.

Well you got to. Why do you think you're at the water every day? Why do you think you want to walk into the water like Virginia Woolf with her dress full of rocks? You gotta let the anchors go, get free from your chains.

I don't know how!

I screamed this
at her, the
force of my
voice shocking me.
She nodded again
and came towards
me, holding out
her hands. I
wasn't afraid of
her, I didn't
back away. I
welcomed her touch.
Let me help you.
She laid her
hands on the
arm that held
the tattoos and
a warmth spread
from her touch.
It spread up
my arm and
into me, as
if her heat
were a living
thing. The anchors
on my arm
began to shift
on my skin,
as if the tattoos

were melting off
of my me.
The heat from
her touch increased
and I heard another
clang of chains
and the flapping
of wings. I
looked at the
tattoos as they
began to change
and morph. I
heard more fluttering
of wings and
nearly screamed when
the first anchor
tattoo became a
small black crow.
It lifted off
my skin and
grew larger It
stayed there in
the air and
looked at me
for a moment
before flying away.
Six more crows
came after the
first one and

when each one
left my skin,
the clang jangle
of chains grew
louder until it
sounded like music.
I watched as
each of the
crows flew away
into the air
and marvelled at
how light I
felt, how free.
When they were
gone, the music
of the chains
ceased and I
could see them,
like long snakes
twisting along the
sand. They shone
bright, burning red
as if they were
being heated by
fire and then
blew apart into
dust that shone
like diamonds. I
was silent for

a moment, marvelling
at the gift
the woman had
given me, at
her kindness. I
looked at her.
Why did you do this for me? Is there anything I can do for you?
She gave me
another laugh and
instead of ruffling
my feathers, the
sound filled me
with light. When
she took her
hand away, I
still felt her
warmth inside me.
**Just go on and live your life honey. Besides, I didn't want you
to end up like me.**
She touched my
cheek and gave
me another smile
and turned from
me. She walked
into the water
and seemed to
float on it
for an instant
before her form

began to fade
and all that
was left of
her was taken
by the waves.

A Foundation of Trees

* For my Wonder Dad

I am thankful for
what you've given me.
You've taught me
about forgiveness
and how to let go
of past mistakes.
You've shown me
what love really is
and how to nurture it
and make it grow.
You've given me
examples on how
to really live my life,
each one more precious
than the shiniest jewel.
The foundations you've
taught me over the years
have prospered like trees
that have grown leaves.
They reach for the sky
hoping to touch the sun .
As I continue to live life
to its fullest, the things
you have taught me
remain and I can only

hope that by reaching
for the sky on my own
that I do you proud
and keep the trees growing
until they finally
touch the sun.

A Nebulous of Words

I dream of you while I sleep.
In the dream, you take my hand
and hold it, letting your warmth
slip up my arm and into my heart.
Neither of us says anything
because there are no words
to describe what lies between us.
When I wake, I try to think
of some words and find them
all lacking, not quite enough,
but they will have to do.
I utter each word like a wish
and hope that they will find you,
travel to you over the sea,
and come to you in your slumber.
I sit outside, letting the sun
shine down on my face,
reminiscent of the warmth
and the fire that you awake
inside of me. I speak each word
softly as if it is a prayer or hope
given voice. As I speak each word,
shape each syllable, I watch
as it slides out of my mouth
and forms a small ball of light,
an embodiment of the joy
that you fill me with.

They travel around me
like small suns, rotating
in orbit. When I'm done
and the last word is spoken,
they rise into the air and slip
away from me, leaving trails
of light in the air. I know that
when they find you, they
will not be small suns, but
a nebulous of stars that
will shine brightly, marking
your path through the sky
and guiding you back
to me, each word a star
that you can wish upon
as you find your way
home.

The Masks We Wear

I used to
know someone who
insisted we wore
many masks in
our lives. We
wore one mask
at work, a
different one with
friends, another with
lovers, one more
with parents. I
imagined a closet
filled with all
sorts of different
masks instead of
shoes or clothes.

"I don't wear masks."

I told him.

"It's easier that way."

He became belligerent.

"Everyone wears masks! How else would we survive?"

I looked at
him with the
strange feeling that
I didn't really
know him. I
wondered what kind

of mask he
wore with me.

   "Would you behave the same way at work as you do at home?"
He asked me.
I nodded yes.

"I am always myself."
He scoffed at
me, his tone
full of derision.

   "Please. At work, you wear a professional mask. At home, you
wear another."
We agreed to
disagree. I thought
he had the
wrong of it,
that you didn't
have to wear
masks to get
through life. I
pointed out that
you could be
yourself, but just
another fraction of
who you were.

   "So it's a partial mask. That's all it is. I'm wearing a mask with
you."
He said. I
was shocked as
I hadn't known

he needed a
mask to be
around me. I
asked him quietly:
"What mask do you wear around me?"
He scoffed again.

"You don't want to know."

He was right.
I didn't want
to know. Later,
I searched my
face for a
mask, a crack
that ran along
my skin. I
saw a thin
line that ran
along the edge
of my face,
down along my
jaw. It was
a thin mask,
almost like glass
made supple and
bendable. It was
almost me, but
I was still
hiding. Still locking
my true self

behind another face.
I dug my
fingers under the
edge and gently
pulled. The mask
came away easily,
the glue holding
it on turned
dry. I wondered
if I had left
it on whether
it would have
just melted away
on its own.
When the mask
was free, I
looked at myself.
There was a
light that shone
from my skin,
bright like the
morning sun. I
thought that this
was why I
had worn the
mask, so as
not to make
him uncomfortable with
my light, as

he didn't have
one. He didn't
shine. I resolved
to find someone
else who shone,
who burned brightly.
I went out
into the world,
without a mask,
to see what
I could see.
Other men wore
blue masks, grey
masks, red masks.
They carried the
marks of their
souls on the
surface. They
were hiding behind
themselves. They were
locked behind their
fears, their worries,
their perceived weaknesses.
They didn't just
wear them as
masks, but as
shrouds, mantles and
cloaks. The only
difference between them

and myself was
that I no
longer wanted to
wear a mantle
of needles. I
wanted to live
as myself, not
behind my pain.
They weren't ready
to shine as
themselves. I despaired
about ever finding
someone who wore
no masks and
had given up.
It was when
I had given
up that he
found me. I
walked into the
coffee shop, not
thinking anything would
happen but when
he turned towards
me, I was
struck by the
light that poured
from him. I
stood there for

a moment, searching
his face for
a mask, for that
tell-tale sheen of
glass that ran
along his skin.
There wasn't one.

<u>"Hi."</u>

He said. I
was almost speechless,
unable to find
words accurate enough
for an introduction.

"Hi."

I said, thinking
that the word
was lacking. I
had finally found
someone who didn't
wear a mask,
or he had
found me. That
didn't matter. What
did was that
we had found
each other. There
were no coloured
masks on his
face, no blues

or reds or
black glass or
or green. There
was only him,
shining brightly like
a star or sun.
There was only
him. He smiled
and the light
from inside him
grew only brighter.
My light glowed
in response and
the air hummed
with possibilities.

<u>Holding the Chalice Tightly</u>

Everyone has a
chalice inside of
them. That glass
barrier that lies
between body and
spirit. Over time,
the chalice can
break and crack.
I was forever
picking up pieces
of mine. I
would be walking
along and hear
the soft clink
of glass behind
me. I would
pick up the
shard of glass
and let it
sit in my
hand for a
moment as it
caught the light.
Then, slowly, it
would sink back
into my flesh.
It never found

it's proper place
though, so when
I walked, it
sounded like bells
were singing as
I moved. I
healed my body,
mind and spirit
but the chalice
still remained in
pieces. Though I
was whole on
the outside, I
was still in
pieces. I didn't
think the chalice
would be whole
again. Until I
met him. As
our feelings grew,
I could feel
the pieces of
the chalice moving
inside of me,
finding their rightful
place, forming the
chalice once more.
They were in
place, waiting for

the moment. When
he told me
that he loved
me for the
very first time,
and I told him
the same, he
pulled me into
a tight embrace.
Rather than break
the chalice, I
could feel the
pieces melding back
together, fusing and
forming. A new music
began to play
from inside of
me. It was
the sound of
bells, made from
a whole chalice
rather than a
broken one. It
began filling me
with light and
love for him.
He looked at
me and said
"I love you."

The music of
the bells grew
until the world
around us was
filled with light
"I love you, too."
I said. Light
poured from both
of us and
danced to the
sound of music
and I was
complete once more.

A Language Upon the Leaves

You helped me relearn a language unknown
something primal and unspoken.
Our love has bloomed and has grown,
a seed beginning to spring open.
The language you taught me once again
was one that I'd forgotten.
Every touch, caress and every when,
is but a new leaf begotten.
Inside my heart, the language you speak
is written upon the leaves.
The bird takes them in his beak
and brings them to the breeze.
The tree we planted and nurtured still grows
and whispers the words every time the wind blows.

<u>My Life is Up to Me</u>

I was lost
inside of myself.
I had forgotten
what it was
to actually live.
I had given
up, had chosen
to hide in
the dark. It
wasn't as painful
as the light.
I had given
up. I was
raised not to
be a quitter,
but I could
see no other
way, could not
see around the
dark mountain inside
of my head.
I lay down
that night to
sleep and prayed
for it to
be endless, to
not wake up.

I prayed so
hard that tears
coursed down my
face while sleep
laid its claim
on my body.
I woke to a
noise in the
kitchen. I got
out of bed
and walked toward
the noise. My
grandmother, long ago
dead, stood making
a jug of
pink lemonade. She
heard me and
turned, a smile
upon her face.
**Better drink up while it's still cold. If it gets warm, it tastes like
piss.**
Her smile deepened
and she held
out a glass
to me. I
took it, my
hands shaking slightly.
How can you be here?
I asked her.

You died when I was eight.
She smiled and
motioned at my
glass of pink
lemonade, almost
waving at it.
**Aren't you going to drink it? I came a long way to make it for
you.**
I took a sip
and the tart
sweetness of it
flooded my mouth.
**Now, listen. You need some sense knocked into you. You can't
keep living like this.**
How else can I live?
**You can stop being sorry for yourself for one thing. You can
get out there and live.**
I don't know how.
She gave me
a look that
I remembered well.
It was a
look that said
you had better
pay close attention.
**You were doing fine before. Now you've been given another
chance, and you're choosing to spend it in darkness?**
I tried to
think of everything

I was feeling,

all that I

wanted to say.

I don't know how to do anything else. I'm lost.

So find yourself again. It's a simple change to make, a simple fix.

I don't know how.

She sighed and

poured herself a

glass of lemonade.

Her stare softened.

She took a

sip and spoke

oh so softly.

Look, I know what's happened to you is hard. And I know that change is hard, that it sometimes takes everything you have. You have to make a change for the better.

I don't know how.

You keep saying that, but why do you have this?

She pointed at

a small magnet

on my fridge.

It was bright

yellow and had

six small words,

six syllables that

resounded, loud and

strong, even through

my current haze.

My life is up to me.
The words sounded
almost like music
coming from my
lips. My grandmother
nodded, smiling kindly.
Who gave you that magnet?
My mother.
**Smart woman, your mother. Always liked her. You need to
remember those words, every time you're afraid of making a
change. Say the words again.**
I nodded and
did so. My
voice was still
soft and quiet.
My life is up to me.
**No, no, that's not working. Why are you living in such a dark
place? You need a little light.**
My grandmother snapped
her fingers and
the magnet began
to pulse softly
with light, shining
from the fridge.
Now say the words again.
My life is up to me.
The light from
the magnet grew
a little brighter.

138

And now say it again, but mean it this time, shout it!
My life is up to me!
The light increased
until it was
almost blinding. I
had to shield
my eyes from
its brilliance. I
heard my grandmother's
voice again. She
sounded far away now.
Never forget, you control what changes in your life. That's
what gives you courage. I am so proud of you.
The light grew
even brighter, more
luminous. I had
to close my
eyes. When I
opened them again,
I was in
my bedroom, still
in bed. I
shook myself awake,
filled with an
emptiness that just
wanted to be filled.
It was a dream.
I said, not
wanting it to

be so. It
had seemed so
real, so true.
I got out
of bed and
walked into the
kitchen. There, sitting
on the counter,
was a jug
filled with pink
lemonade and two
glasses, half full.
I looked around.
Grandmother?
I said. My voice
was soft. I heard
a sound that
was like the
snapping of fingers.
I turned and
looked at the
fridge. There, the
little magnet with
six simple words
was glowing bright
like the sun.
My life is up to me.
I said, my
voice finding strength.

My life is up to me.

The Mind Garden

I came upon
a doorway. It
was tall and
narrow and was
made from old
wood painted red
that had faded
over time in
the sun. The
doorway was unremarkable
except for two
reasons: It stood
in the middle
of a parking
lot and from
the open door
there came the
sound of laughter.
A boy came
out and looked
at me. He wore
round glasses and
had a dark brown
mop of hair.
He smiled, the
smile filled with

gaps. He let out
another loud laugh.
"Do you want to come see the garden?"
I looked around to
see if the
boy's parents were
around, but there was
no one. He
laughed loudly again.
"Don't be afraid. You'll be okay."
"Where are your parents?"
I asked him.
Surely, he wasn't
alone. He grinned.
"They're close. They're your parents! Come on!"
Beckoning with one
hand, he raced
away from the
doorway. He stood,
looking at me,
a smile still
playing upon his
lips. He was standing
in what looked
to be a large
meadow surrounded by
trees. I went
around to the
back of the

143

doorway, but there
was nothing. Only
a brick wall
and some grease
stains. I went
back around to
the front and
looked inside again.
The boy still
stood there, looking
at me with
twinkling, bright eyes.
"Come on! There's nothing to be afraid of!"
I nodded, not
trusting myself to
speak. Stepping over
the threshold of
the door, there
was a loud rushing
sound and my
ears popped from
sudden pressure. Then
I was through,
and my ears
cleared. The boy
reached for my
hand. When our
fingers touched, a
wind began to

144

dance in the
grass and flew
upwards. I looked
at the boy.
"What was that?"
He took his
time before he
answered my question.
"The meadow remembers you. Come on, the garden isn't that far."
He pulled me
along and within
moments, we were
at the entrance
of a small
garden. There were
orchids and roses,
petunias and chrysanthemums,
tiger lilies and
ivy. There were
flowers of every
kind, but they
were all relatively
small, as if
they had just
started to grow.
I looked beyond
the small garden
and saw another
one behind it.

I pointed with
a shaking hand.
"What's over there? What's that garden?"
The boys face
darkened. He looked
sad all of
a sudden, as
if the other
garden held nightmares.
"That's the dead garden. Nothing grows there anymore."
He could see
from my face
that I wanted
to explore it.
So he led
the way, keeping
hold of my
hand. As we
walked, a question
occurred to me.
"If this garden is dead, how did the new one grow?"
The boy laughed
again and the
breeze responded in
kind, laughing among
the grass. The
boy looked at
me with strangely
serious, mature eyes.

146

"Do you really not know?"
I shook my
head, but an
answer came to
me moments before
he said it.
"They come from imagination. From ideas. All you have to do is
think of it and the ideas will grow."
He led on
until we came
to the dead
garden. Its plants
were all dead
and none that
I could name.
It was filled
with spiky plants
that looked as
if they were
ready to draw
blood should we
touch one. I
looked at the
boy, trying to
find my voice.
"Did ideas grow this garden too?"
He nodded, a
tear sliding down
his cheek. He

made no effort
to wipe it
off his face.
"Yours. It was your ideas and imagination that caused both
gardens to grow."
I was shaken
but his words
had the ring
of truth to
them. I asked
the first thing
that came to
mind, letting the
words spill out.
"How could I grow this?"
"You were unhappy. The thoughts that you have hold power.
What's inside your mind takes root in the real world."
"Then why does the other garden exist?"
The boy let
out a hearty
laugh and squeezed
my hand tightly.
"Because you're better now. We're better."
I looked back
at the healthy
garden, so full
of life. Then
I looked at
the dead garden.

"I want you to help me to do something. Will you?"

"Of course."

"If imagination caused this garden, maybe new thoughts, new ideas, will make it better again."

I was pretty
sure I knew
who the boy
was, what he
was. He nodded
and took both
my hands. I
took a deep
breath and imagined
life growing around
us, coming out
of the dark
soil. There was
nothing at first,
but then we
both heard the ground
around us begin
to crack and
rumble. It shook
for a moment
and then grass
shot out of
the ground where
before there was
only black, burnt

earth. Trees shot
up out of
the ground, their
leaves green and
whole. Flowers slid
out of the ground
with small pops,
hundreds of them,
thousands of them.
Gone was the
black earth and
the plants that
looked as if
they would draw
blood. In the
trees, I could
hear birdsong. I
looked down at
the boy, smiling.
"We did it!"
I couldn't help
letting out a
loud, joyful laugh.
He nodded, smiling
"You did it. You did all of this."
I looked at
him, really looked
at him closely.

"You're me, aren't you? My inner child? You look exactly as I did when I was younger. I don't know why I didn't see it before."

He nodded again.

"Because you couldn't."

"Then where are we? Where is this place?"

He gave me

a big grin.

"Would you believe me if I said we're inside your mind?"

I didn't need

to think of

a proper response.

"Yes. I would. It's the only thing that makes sense. But how do I get out?"

"The way you came. Remember, what you imagine is given life and anything is possible."

I turned to

walk back through

the doorway. The

boy didn't move.

"Aren't you coming with me?"

I asked him.

"No, I think I'll stay here for a while longer. Now that you've found me again, I won't ever be far away. Never forget me, Okay?"

"I won't. I promise."

I turned towards

the doorway, the

trees and plants

swaying in a

soft breeze. As
I stepped back
through the doorway,
I looked back
at the boy.
There was my
inner child, playing
amongst the trees
and flowers, with
joy written on
his face and
laughter in his
heart. I closed
the door, knowing
he'd be safe
now and began
to make my
way home again.

People From My Past

We were walking
back from the
coffee shop, drinks
in hand, when
I saw him.
I gestured to
her and made
sure she had
seen. I pointed
to him, saying
That's my ex-husband.
It was the
first time I had
seen him in
six years. Later,
I wondered at
his appearance.
He was but
the latest in
a long line
of people from
my past that
I had seen
recently. I had
come across people
I used to know,
ex-boyfriends, ex-friends, ex-lovers.

153

I was wondering
at my lack
of a reaction,
at the absence
of anger that
I felt, that I
had carried with
me for so
long. I had
worn his cruel
betrayal as if
it were a
hair shirt, or
a stone around
my neck. Instead
of reacting in
anger, I felt
oddly buoyant and
light. I walked
over to her
and asked her:

Why aren't I reacting more? If this were last year, seeing him would have depressed me for the day. I've seen all these people from my past and they aren't affecting me as I thought they would if I ever saw them again.

I paused for
breath and for
what I really
wanted to ask.

What gives?
She looked at
me with that
sage look in
her eyes that
she had and
smiled at me.
You were ready.
She said simply.
You're a lot better now then you were. You've healed. You're a
different person now. You're on the right path and you're going
where you need to. You wouldn't be seeing them otherwise.
I nodded and
thought of all
the emotions that
these people had
caused me, all
the hurt, depression,
sadness, angst, rage,
despair and malaise.
I realised that
what I was
feeling right then
and there was
simple, unequivocal happiness.
I let go
of the pain,
of the heartache,
of the self-degradation,

and stopped judging
myself by how
other people from
my past had
seen me. All
that there was
now is me
as I chose
to be and
the emotion of
happiness. I choose
to be happy.
All the rest
is just stardust
and the possibilities
of the future.

Living Words

I woke one
morning with words
etched into my
skin. I tried to
read them in
mirror, but the
writing was backwards.
My friends noticed
the words and
asked why I
had tattooed myself
with just a
fraction of a
sentence. I woke
the next morning
to find the
words had doubled
on my skin,
snaking down the
inside of my
arm. I went
to the doctors
and they asked
why I had
marked myself with
words. They didn't
understand when I

told them the
words had just
appeared there on
their own. They
sent me home
with a mild
sedative. When I
woke on the
third morning, I
found that both
my arms were
now covered in
looping black words.
I tried to
read them, attempted
to make sense
of what they
said, but I
could not see
all of the
words. Looking in
the mirror, I
saw they had
started to appear
along the back
of my neck.
My mother was
the one who
explained it to

me. She read
the words, running
her fingers along
some of them,
turning my arms
in order to
read others. She
looked at me.
"Don't you recognize this?"
I shook my head
no. I shrugged.
"I haven't been able to see all of them to read them. What does it say?"
"You should know. You wrote them."
I was shocked.
"What do you mean?"
She pointed to
the words that
ran along the
inside of my
arm, then ran
her fingers along.
"As the cards flew from my grasp, I knew I had made the right decision. I was the Broken Man no longer."
She paused for
breath, and to
point to another
set of words.

"And this here? These say: I had let a piece of my past go and looked forward to what the future would bring."

I shook my head,

not knowing what

to say. My

mother took my

hands and held

them in hers.

"Your life is a living poem. A wonderful, exciting, awesome living poem."

I wondered at

her words, at

what they meant.

What the words

on my skin

meant. She could

see my confusion.

"You put so much of yourself in your words, it is only natural that they will mark you even as you mark the page. Do not be afraid of them."

"How do I get the words out of my skin?"

She looked at

me with a

half smile and

that wise look

she got in

her eyes, deep

and somehow comforting.

"Write. More words will come and you will always be marked by them, but you are a living poem. It has always been this way."
I nodded and
pulled a piece
of paper towards
me. I put my
hand down on
the paper and
watched as the words
on my skin
began to slip
and slide off
of it. I
looked at the
page to see
what they had
to say.

We All Belong to the Same House

While I was
getting my coffee
one morning, I
noticed the barista
was wearing a
locket. Looking closer,
I read the
word "Slytherin" in
a flowing script.
Underneath, the serpent
that represented the
house was curled,
as if lying
in wait. I
pointed to it.
"Where did you get that?"
She looked at
me with shrewd
eyes as if
taking stock of
my worth. She
nodded, assessing me
as one who
was completely worthy.
"I got it at Comicon, but I'm sure there is an Etsy shop."
I held up
my right wrist

and showed her

the scar that

was tattooed there.

She reached out

to touch it.

"Is it a real tattoo?"

I nodded, smiling.

Like recognizes like.

"What house are you in? Did you get sorted on Pottermore?"

I nodded, smiling.

"I was one of the first million people allowed to access the site."

"So what house?"

"I got sorted into Ravenclaw, but I think I belong in Gryffindor."

"Oh, no, you have to trust the Sorting Hat. It knows."

"But I have the scar…"

She gave it

another hungry look.

"That's a symbol for the whole series. It's Harry's story, right? But if the Sorting Hat and JK Rowling put you in Ravenclaw, that's where you belong."

I must have

looked put out

so she sang:

"Or yet in wise old Ravenclaw, if you've a ready mind, where those of wit and learning, will always find their kind."

I recognized the

song. It's what

the Sorting Hat

first sung when
Harry was sorted.
She looked at
me with a
strong, searching look.
"Are you wise? Do you crave knowledge? Are you drawn to air?
That's the element associated with Ravenclaw, you know."
Something occurred to
me and I
pointed to the
necklace she wore.
"Were you sorted into Slytherin?"
I asked her.
She nodded, a
spark lighting up
her eyes. They
looked as if
they were filled
with glitter magic.
"Yes, I was. I wasn't happy about it at first, I wanted Gryffindor,
everyone does. But we're all parts of the same house, you know.
However, it's our differences that make us strong."
I wasn't sure
if she was
referring to Harry
Potter, or something
deeper than that.
I took my
coffee and bade

her a nice
day. She put
her hand out,
catching my wrist.
*"Trust in the Sorting Hat. It knows where you belong. We all have
to belong somewhere."*
I nodded and
made my way
to work. I
looked online for
a Ravenclaw necklace.
My acceptance of
my house within
the world of
Harry Potter was
a small thing,
but at the
thought of stretching
my wings like
an eagle, and
soaring into the
air, my heart
soared with it
and I knew
where I belonged.

The Unknown Language of the Heart

My heart was
unable to speak.
It would look
at other people
in love and
wonder what they
were saying to
each other without
speaking. What kind
of unknown language
passed between them?
I despaired of
ever finding someone
who loved me
deeply enough to
speak without speaking,
to touch my
heart with a
simple caress. That
changed when I
met you. The
love between us
grew slowly, starting
as a seed
that was planted
in my heart
the moment we

first kissed. It
was nurtured with
every endearment and
each caress. When
the flower bloomed,
filling me completely,
I heard a
soft buzzing, felt
a throb of
vibration as my
heart began to
respond to yours.
Now, when you
touched me, it
was like you
touched my heart.
Now when you
spoke to me,
it was as
if you spoke
to my soul.
At first, I
was terrified. What
was this unknown
language? What did
it all mean?
You took my
face in your
hands and looked

right into me.
"Don't be afraid."
You said to
me. At those
words, my fear
fell away and
a series of
words I had
not known began
to show themselves
appearing as if
something was rubbed
away and the
words were there
the entire time.
All they needed
was someone to
help me see
them. Now when
you look at
me, the words
from the unknown
language become known
all over again.
All it took
was your love
to set the
words, and myself,
free.

A Waking Dream

I hadn't slept
in days. I
would lay awake
at night, waiting
for sleep to
come, but it
wouldn't. I would
take warm baths,
drink herbal tea,
but sleep still
eluded me. It
had been seven
days since I
had known sleeps
embrace and I
was starting to
lose it, even
though I didn't
know what "it"
was. I started
to see things,
objects and people
that couldn't possibly
be there, while
I was awake.
The shadows of
the waking dreams

moved along my
bedroom walls, along
the sidewalks,
showed their reflections
upon store windows.
The mirror people
would glare at
me as I
passed by, watching
me, almost as
if they were
measuring my worth.
The mannequins would
move closer to
the windows, hoping
to catch a
glimpse of me
through the reflections
that shouldn't be
there but were.
Then the unthinkable
happened. In bed
one night, waiting,
hoping, praying for
sleep, I watched
as the shadows
moved and slithered.
They whispered as
they moved along

the walls. I
watched them as
they shaped themselves
into an arch
of branches. There
were thorns running
along them. Even
though they were
merely shadows, I
knew they would
draw blood. In
front of the
arch was a
sign that merely
said three words:
Sleep, This Way.
I knew I
would have to
walk through the
arch. I gathered
up my courage
and walked through
the thorns. Breathing
deeply, I did
so, feeling the
bite and caress
of the thorns
and brambles. There
was darkness for

a moment, just
for a second and
the smell of
sweat and age,
rot and filth.
When my eyes
cleared, I found
myself in an
alley. There was
but one light
that hung high
up on one
wall, flickering like
a candle flame.
I could see
shadows along the
ground, shapes that
I knew were
other people. I
wondered if any
of them were
the reflections, the
dream people that
had watched me.
I walked down
the alley, the
arch of thorns
having disappeared. Several
of these shapes

called out to
me in pained,
gruff, angry voices,
men and women,
the lost people.
"I didn't do what they said. You gotta believe me. I didn't."
"I need a drink real bad, just one drink. Any drink."
"I used to be so pretty, so pretty. I could have my pick of men."
**"I didn't mean to kill her, but she was asking for it. So was
he."**
*"You gotta wear a foil hat, man. Otherwise they can hear your
thoughts. "*
"I'm so hungry. Spare a bite to eat?"
I walked on,
faster, faster, faster.
The alley and
the forgotten went
on forever and
my footsteps were
loud in the
darkness, each step
a crunch of
gravel, glass or
stone, each grab
of their hands
like the thorns
on the arch
I had walked
though to get

here. I pulled
myself away and
broke into a
run, trying to
find the end
of the alley.
The light was
flickering madly off
of the brick
walls and there
was no ending
in sight that
I could see.
Then, in front
of me, a
shadow person stood,
detaching himself from
the mass of moving
thorn people. He
held out his
hands, telling me
to stop without
words. I tried
to run past
him, but he
grabbed hold of
me, held tight
until I stopped
struggling. The entire

time it took
me to calm
down he was
talking to me:

"It's okay man, it's okay. I'm not going to hurt you, I'm not going to hurt you. It's okay."

I stopped and
looked at him.
He was grimy
and covered in
filth like the
rest of them
but there was
clarity in his
face. He smiled
at me and,
despite my fear,
I smiled back.

"You're going about this all wrong, you know."

"What do you mean?"

My voice echoed
off the walls.

"You can keep running forever, if you want to. Makes no difference to me."

"What else can I do?"

"Well, you can focus on the person who's dreaming of you for starters."

"But I'm not sleeping."

"I know. Legend says that when you can't sleep, someone else is dreaming about you and you're awake in that person's dream."

"That doesn't make sense."

"Does any of this?"

He motioned around

us at the

walls and the

flickering light, at

the mass of

shadows that were

people. He gave

me another grin.

"This is where your nightmares come from. Dreams don't make any sense. They are pieces of our life we've already lived."

I found myself

nodding, knowing he

was speaking truth.

"So what do I do? How do I leave this place?"

"Well now, that's simple. You have to focus on the person who's dreaming of you and go to them."

"I can do that?"

"Sure. It's your dream, isn't it?"

I turned around

in a circle,

looking at the

shadows. I turned

back to the

man, his eyes
bright and his
smile warm, comforting.

"How do I find the other person? I don't know how to get back the way I came."

"You wouldn't want to. No, your way to him is simple. See that light?"

He pointed to
the light, the
only source of
brightness in amongst
all the shadows.

"That's him. He's been watching over you all this time, you know. Even in the darkest of times, he's there."

"How do I go to him?"

"Haven't you figured it out yet? Close your eyes, think on the light. Don't think about anything else. Go towards the light."

"Is that like dying?"

He shook his
head back and
forth, laughing and
smiling at me.

"Well, they do call sleep the little death."

He said, thoughtfully.

"This is a dream, not some horror movie. Some dreams end and some dreams become a reality. That's the great thing. So just focus on the light, nothing else."

I did as
he said and

closed my eyes.
I thought of
the light, pictured
it growing brighter.
I could see
the brightness
of the light
growing, even with
my eyes closed,
could even begin
to feel the
heat of it
on my face.
Soon, the fetid
air disappeared and
was replaced with
the smell of
a spicy cologne
and the scent
of honeysuckle. I
heard movement as
someone moved towards
me. I would
not be afraid.
A voice said:
"Open your eyes."
I did and
saw him and
the feeling of

the light upon
my face flowed
through my whole
body. The light
came from him.
"I dreamt of you."
He said. I
smiled at him.
"I know."
I said softly.
Then words weren't
necessary. There was
only me, only
him, only us
and the gorgeous
possibility of dream.

I am a Bisexual Moose

When I first
knew what I
was, the secret
inside of me,
I was at
university, a world
away from home.
We were in
the unicentre cafeteria,
a whole group
of us. We all
rotated around one
girl, Sheenagh. She
was our light.
I sat next
to her and
she could tell
that something was
bothering me. Artists,
whether into literature,
music or theatre
can always sense
discontent. She
gave me one
of her patented
Sheenagh looks, where
you wondered what

she would say.

"What's wrong with you? Are you on your man rag?"

She gave me

a Sheenagh smile,

and her brightness

increased. I wanted

to shine just

as brightly as

she did, but

for now, I

was content to

be in her

orbit. I struggled

with the words

I had to

say, words that

I had been

holding in for

as long as

I could remember.

I was nearly

shaking. Sheenagh

saw this and

put a hand

on my arm.

"What is it, honey? Don't be afraid of what you need to say."

I swallowed thickly.

"I think I'm gay."

The world did

not stop and

no one ran

screaming from the

building. She laughed.

"Oh honey, I don't think you're gay. I know you are. Say it again.
Own those words and be proud of who you are."

I nodded and

gathered my voice.

"I'm gay."

She laughed again,

the sound like

a tinkle of

bells being caressed

by water. Sheenagh

touched my cheek.

"You're so serious. It's not a serious thing, it's a glorious thing,
becoming yourself. Am I the first person you've told?"

I nodded again.

"Oh, sweetheart. I'm honoured. What's your favourite animal?"

I though about

it for a

moment. It had

been cows up

until recently, but

lately, Wolves had

been entering my

dreams at night.

"Wolves."

I said, smiling.

"There now. We have to celebrate your freedom!"

"My freedom?"

"Yes! You're free from your past and your life begins now!"

She stood up

on her chair

and then got

onto the table.

She raised her

arms up in

the air and

spoke in a

loud voice that

carried through the

whole unicentre cafeteria.

"I am a bisexual moose!"

I expected the

others to laugh,

for the crowd

around us to

tell us to

shut up, for

someone to complain.

Instead, one of

the other people

who orbited around

Sheenagh, another artist

named Jackie, stood

up, and proclaimed:

"I am a lesbian porpoise!"

Others were getting
into the spirit
of things, climbing
onto their tables
and proclaiming what
they were for
everyone to hear.
"I am a gay lion"
"I am a lesbian tiger!"
"I am a bisexual bear!"
"I am a straight fish!"
"I am a lesbian gorilla!"
"I am an asexual dog!"
"I am a straight cat!"
"I am a gay chinchilla!"
"I am a lesbian cougar!"
I was the
last one, the
only one who
hadn't stood up
on the table
and proclaimed to
the world who
and what I
was. Sheenagh held
out her hand
to me, smiling.
"It's your turn honey. Shine bright and do not be afraid of who you are."

I stood and
climbed up onto
my chair, I
took her hand
and got up
onto the table.
"I am a gay Wolf."
I said quietly.
"Oh, no, honey. You have to yell it. Wolves aren't quiet like mice,
they howl at the moon! You have to howl it honey, howl!"
"I AM A GAY WOLF!"
I screamed. Tears
were sliding down
my cheeks and
I felt a
moment of release,
of weightlessness. I
looked at Sheenagh
and she was
shining bright like
the sun she
was. She looked
at me with
eyes that were
so incredibly wise.
"There now. That wasn't so hard, was it? I'm proud of you, my
little Wolf."
Everyone around us
began clapping and

cheering. In that
moment, I was
free. After university,
I never saw
Sheenagh again, but
I've followed her
example and have
continued shining brightly.

Music, Bells and Birdsong

There aren't enough words...
I told him.
He looked at
me with a
smile that radiated
warmth. He took
my hand and
I felt that
warmth from him
pass into me.
There doesn't have to be words. I know how you feel in here.
He pointed to
his heart. Then
to his eyes.
I see it, every time I look at you.
I know, I feel the same way.
I said. However,
he could see
that I still
wanted to find
the words. It
was what I
did. I was
always able to
describe the indescribable.
With him, I
found words lacking.

Tell me what you would say. Not with words, but with emotions.
I thought that
to be an
impossible task. He
could see that
I was having
trouble trying to
put into words
that which I
couldn't describe. He
took my hand.
Just try.
He said softly.
For me.
I nodded and
tried to picture
what he made
me feel like.
I saw warm
sun shining on
my skin, bright
like the warmth
that he filled
me with. I
opened my eyes
and saw nothing
had change. He
took my other
hand and smiled.

You have to give life to what you see. Use your imagination.
I opened my
mouth to respond
and a ball
of light slipped
out of my
mouth. It floated
between us for
a moment before
rising to the
sky, filling the
world around us
with light. He
smiled at me.
There, I knew you could do it. What else do you see?
I thought of
how he was
like the breeze
flowing through the
trees, how just
the touch of
him made me
feel alive. Around
us, shoots began
to slide out
of the grass,
forming a circle
of trees around
us. He laughed

at this and
the sound was
like music to
my ears. He
moved closer to
me, put his
arm around me.
What else?
I thought of
how his love
for me filled
my heart with
song. I heard
the flutter of
wings and we
looked up into
the branches of
the trees and
they were filled
with birds of
every shape and
colour. They sang
sweetly to us,
a melody that
made my body
lighter. He kissed
me, softly and
looked at me,
so deep that

I thought I
could see his
soul, as if
his eyes were
windows or doorways.
You're perfect.
I shook my
head, letting out
a laugh that
was its own
kind of music.
I'm far from perfect.
You're perfect to me and I love all of you.
I let out
a happy sigh
and that turned
into a wind
that set the
leaves moving. The
sound was like
bells ringing and
I kissed him
amongst the music
of bells and
birdsong.

<u>Letting It Go</u>

The anger still
tries to raise
its ugly head
within me. When
the dragon roars,
it is as
if I am
viewing myself from
a distance above
my head, looking
down. I'm watching
myself and don't
recognize myself, what
I become when
I've lost myself
in pure emotion.
I always come
back to myself,
so that I
can see out
of my own
eyes once more.
When I come
back to myself,
I look around
at the fires
that I started

with my own
breath, with my
wordless wails of
woe and rage.
Afterwards, I sit
and remember to
breathe. This time,
I need the
wind on my
face, the earth
under my feet.
I find a
bench by a
city street and
sit there, letting
the world pass
me by. I
begin to cry,
the tears sliding
down my face.
Soon, the tears
pool at my
feet. The puddle
begins to grow,
the tears forming
first a stream
and then a
river where the
road used to

be. The drivers
ride along the
waves as if
nothing is wrong.
I realize that
I am the
only one who
can see the
water. Its waves
lap against my
feet. I hear
a voice inside
speaking softly, gently,
in my ear:
"Let it go."
I open my
mouth and tilt
my head to
the sky. Leaves
pour out of
my mouth, each
of them pointy
and black in
colour. There are
tinges of red
along the edges.
As each leaf
leaves my mouth,
it rides along

the air for
a moment before
landing in the
water. The leaves
make ripples in
the water that
radiate outward. Soon
the water is
filled with leaves,
a sea of
them. As each
leaf hits the
water, I feel
lighter, as if
I'm regaining a
part of myself.
Soon, the flow
of leaves from
my mouth slows
and then stops.
I simply watch
as the leaves
are taken away
by the water
that only I
can see.

Skin Chrysalis

It was the
same every year.
The day after
my birthday, a
thin crust would
begin to form
on my skin.
Throughout the year,
it would grow
tougher, as if
made from stone
or marble. It
would grow thicker,
It would become
more difficult to
move as the
year passed on,
harder to move
my body as
I wanted to.
The evening before
my birthday, the
crust would begin
to crack and
break, flaking off
and falling to
the floor. I

would sweep the
pile of dust
up off the
floor and place
it in a
small cloth bag.
I don't know
why I kept
the dust, why
I held onto
it. I only
knew It felt
right somehow, like
it was expected.
This year's dust
was different. The
layer of thickness
that covered my
skin began to
break and crack
the evening before
my birthday. However,
when the shell
that had made
a mould of
my body began
to break, it
slipped free to
reveal something different

about my body.
I had wings.
They were tattooed
along my skin
but if I focused
on flying, they
slipped out of
my skin and
would flutter in
the air and
I would rise
up a few
feet. When I
didn't want to
fly, they would
rest once again
along my skin,
simple lines of
ink. I panicked,
wondering what was
wrong with me.
I gathered up
my cloth bags
of dust and
brought them to
a wise woman.
"Can you tell me what's wrong with me?"
She looked at
the tattooed wings,

ran her fingers
along them. I
made the wings
flutter for her.
She then looked
at the bags
of dust. I
looked at her.
"This was not made from a shell as you describe."
"What was it then?"
She looked at
me with eyes
that were a
deep, dark brown.
"It was a chrysalis."
Her words sent
my wings fluttering
anew. It seemed
that they agreed
with her assessment.
"I don't understand. It's always been just a shell before. Why
now?"
She put her
fingers in the
most recent cloth
bag and took
them out. Pinched
between her fingers
was a glittering

powder. She let
it trickle from
her fingers and
it glittered in
the soft light.
"Would a shell produce this? As to why now? Well, the butterfly
goes through several stages. The Chrysalis is just one of them."
I shook my
head in bewilderment.
"Why now?"
Her brown eyes
saw so much.
They saw right
into the core
of my heart.
"Because you were ready."
"I don't understand what I'm supposed to do."
She laughed lightly
and the sound
was calming instead
of being jarring.
"Isn't it obvious? What does a butterfly do when it leaves its
chrysalis?"
I shook my
head, not knowing
how to respond.
She simply said:
"It flies."

Poker Symptoms

The room was
filled with smoke
when I came
in. They all
looked up at
me: Frank Fatigue,
Bob Balance, Steven
Speech. Travis Tremors,
Brian Brain Fog.
Sergio Spasm was
there too as
well as two
other shadowy shapes.
I looked at
all of them
and wished all
of them away.
Seven could see
the look of
distaste I wore.
"Come on, don't be that way. Take a seat. We're playing poker."
I grumbled something
about needing a
cup of tea,
but Brian waved
a hand at
me. He let

out a laugh.

"Come on, it won't take long. We'll make it a short game. What's the harm?"

The harm was
that I didn't
like any of
them, that I
wanted all of
them to go
away and leave
me as I
was, as I
had been. Brian
was especially perceptive,
and I knew
he could read
my mind, having
shared so much
of it with
me. He nodded.

"We don't like it much either. You'll have to take that up with Max Shadow."

One of the
shadow shapes moved
into the light
and I saw
Max Shadow for
the first time.
He was thin

with pallid skin
and long greasy
hair. He looked
like what I
imagined Flagg from
the Stand would
look like. He
smiled at me.
"Did someone say my name?"
He said, his
voice as oily
as his hair.
The other shadow
moved into sight
and I saw Cedric
Paulson for the
first time. He
looked like me
from a younger
age, but stretched
into adulthood, as
if he was
not fully in
control of his
thin limbs. He
looked as if
a stiff wind
would knock him
over and his

hands were shaking.

"Well, if you're playing, so am I."

He said. His
voice sounded unsure
of itself, as
if he was
not used to
standing up for
himself. He sighed
and his shoulders
dropped, though the
rest of him
still shook slightly.

"That is, if there's room."

"Of course there's room."

Travis said. His
voice was cheerful,
even though it
shook. He gave
me a smile.

"Come on, we saved a seat just for you."

Sergio motioned with
his hand, also
smiling at me.

"Come on, it's a good seat. Look, I have a cup of tea right here."

He reached for
a cup on the
table, but his back
chose that moment

to seize up
and when he
spoke next, it
was with obvious
pain. I motioned
to Sergio flippantly.
"Will he be all right?"
Max Shadow gave
me an oily
smile and a
small mirthless laugh.
"Of course he will. You're okay, aren't you?"
I didn't know
how to answer
that question, so
moved through the
fog of smoke
and took my
seat. They watched
me as if
afraid I would
bolt from my
chair and run
from the room.
They all puffed
smoke out of
their mouths. I
did not, but
watched as the

smoke formed animals,
like each one
of them had
a Patronus of
some kind, an
animal that represented
their force. I
coughed and waved
my hand through
the smoke. Cedric
let out a
laugh and passed
me the deck
of cards. He
motioned to me.
"It's your turn to deal."
I took the
cards in my
hand and went
to shuffle them.
It was then
that I saw
they weren't playing
cards. They were
tarot cards. I
looked up at
all of them,
not understanding. They
looked back at

me. Finally, from
inside a cloud
of smoke, Max
Shadow spoke softly.

"The game is simple, really. Draw five cards and see what they have to say."

"What kind of poker is this?"

"Well, the stakes are a little high, I'm afraid."

He smiled, his
teeth shining through
the smoke, and
held out his
hands to the
side, as if
to say mea
culpa. He motioned
to the cards.

"You just have to see what they say. We'll all be playing along with you."

"How is that possible?"

"We're part of you and anything is possible. Haven't you figured that out by now?"

I blinked my
eyes and they
were gone from
the room. However,
I could feel
them in me:
Frank, Bob, Steven,

Travis, Brian, Sergio.
Max and Cedric
were there too.
They were all
looking through my
eyes. I sighed
and shuffled the
cards, thinking my
question silently. I
closed my eyes,
just for a
moment. Then I
drew three cards
and looked down
at what the
cards had to
say.

Candlelight and Three Simple Words

You have lit
a candle inside
of me. With
every touch, each
caress, each brush
of your lips
against mine,
the flame grows.
I had thought
the flame to
be extinguished, only
a mere finger
of smoke that
moved and undulated
inside me. Now,
the tiny tongue
of flame is
a light all
its own inside
of me. Every
time you tell
me those three
simple words with
a precious magic
all their own,
(I love you)
each word like

a caress along
my heart, the
flame grows brighter
still until I
am filled to
the brim with
love and light
for you.

Joy Given Shape

* For Rachael, because you are wonderful.

When I look
at you, all
I see is
light. Every movement
you make leaves
tracers in the
air, so bright
and beautiful is
the light that
pulsates from you.
When you speak,
It is as
If you're singing
to a part
of me that
has remained in
the dark and
was waiting to
bask in your
light. You are
joy given shape,
brilliance given focus,
beauty given form
and I am

grateful to know
you.

What Forever Would Bring

When I left
the dark forest,
I walked along
a path. I
didn't know where
it was going,
had no idea
where I would
end up. Above
me, the clouds
changed shape. I
saw eagles, falcons
and other birds,
as if the
very clouds were
telling me to
fly. I made
my way through
the storm fields,
forcing myself to
walk through the
tall grass that
was whipped to
and fro with
such wicked ferocity.
A field of
grass that whispered

thoughts I had
when darkness took
hold. The grass
told me to
lie down within
it, and just
to let go.
I traversed through
the deep, shadowed
murky swamp, ignoring
the goblin that
hid within telling
me that everything
would be okay
if I just stopped trying.
He laughed
at me, at
what I had
been, every terrible
thought I'd had
about myself. I
came to the
ghost lands, where
all those I'd
thought I had
loved called out
to me, telling
that I was
nothing, that I

was pathetic, that
they owned me.
I ignored all
of them, the
grass, the goblin
and the ghosts.
I left them
behind me, in
my past. Instead,
I kept my
eyes on the
path and looked
from time to
time at the
birds in the
sky, leading me
towards what, I
didn't know. The
path turned to
red dust and
pieces of rock.
I suddenly found
myself in front
of a large
mountain that towered
high up into
the sky and
the clouds. There
was no way

I could climb
over it. I
stood there, not
knowing what to
do. It was
then that a
shadow detached itself
from the rocks
and walked towards
I watched as
the shadow grew
bright, as if
it was not
made from darkness
but from a
bright white light.
Then you were
in front of
me, shining like
the stars and
the moon. You
smiled and spoke
my name softly.
"I've been waiting my whole life for you."
You said to
me. I nodded.
"And I for you."
I said. I
pointed to the

mountain, at it blocking the

only way forward.

"What do we do now? How do we climb over it?"

You looked at

the mountain and

then back at me.

"It's only an obstacle because you see it that way. Why don't we just go around?"

I shook my

head, trying to

find the words.

"It could take forever to go around the mountain."

You smiled and

your light increased.

"Then it will be forever with you. Besides, who knows what sights we'll see?"

You took my

hand and we

started off, around

the mountain. The

falcons and the

eagles, the ravens

and the crows,

all made of

clouds but somehow

solid, swooped down

to join us,

following us on

our journey towards

what forever would
bring.

Actual Magic

There are some days
when I feel like
the Scarecrow:
made of straw and
bits of fluff, with my
head filled with clouds,
nary a thought inside,
or able to pass through
the fog that waits within.
On other days, I feel
like the Cowardly Lion,
all bluster, filled with
pomp and circumstance
on the outside to hide
the fatigue and that
all I want is to curl up
and lose myself in slumber.
There are even days
where I feel like
the Tin Man, that metal
being without a heart,
as if emotion can't penetrate
my metal shell, nor
seep through it.
More often than not, though,
I'm looking around at
the world like Dorothy:

full of wonder, enchanted
by the land around me;
being daring enough
to explore everything,
to discover all that life
has to offer, all over again
as if for the first time.
Dorothy held onto the hope
that she would get home,
that she would find the place
in this world and the one
beyond where she belonged.
Though I embody all of them
(the Scarecrow, the Cowardly Lion,
and the Tin Man)
it is Dorothy I hold closest
for she proved two things:
there's no place like home
and that magic,
true magic,
actual magic,
is always possible.

<u>The Lady of Leaves</u>

The leaves had
started to change
colour. No longer
green, they were
filled with hues
of red and
gold and orange.
The world was
once again moving
towards a rainbow
of colour and
there was a
crispness to the
air that smelled
of wood smoke
and hints of
the coming cold.
I came upon
a line of
leaves, leading into
the distance. They
were all the
same brilliant yellow,
so bright it
almost hurt to
look at them.
With the leaves

forming a path,
they looked as
if someone had
taken the bricks
of the yellow
brick road and
arranged them. I
was going to
walk by them
when a wind
rose up around
me, causing the
leaves to circle
and dance around
me. I heard the
crinkle of leaves
and watched as
a woman, dressed
in a dress
the same colour
of the leaves
came walking down
the path towards
me. It was
only as the
cyclone of leaves
ceased it's movement
that I realized
her dress was

made from the
leaves themselves. She
smiled at me
in a kindly
sort of way.
"The leaves normally do not react that way towards your kind."
She said. Her
voice sounded like
the wind rustling
through the trees.
"They've told me to take you with me. Come."
She held out
her hand and
I took it.
The skin was
dry under my
touch and I
wondered why I
was going with
her so willingly;
but there didn't
seem to be
anything to fear
from her. There
was an almost
regal presence to
her and I
felt comfortable immediately.
Her skin was

like paper under
my own. She
saw that I
had questions. My
eyes gave me
away. She smiled
kindly and began
to walk down
the path, bringing
me with her.

*"All will be told in time. Your curiosity is good though, it will serve
you well."*

She walked slowly,
as if every
step was somehow
painful. Indeed, she
was almost limping.

"How will my curiosity serve me well?"

*"Oh, curiosity keeps the spirit alive. When there are always things
to look at, to see, to discover, the soul and spirit grow. It's the
natural way of things."*

She stumbled then
and crumpled to
the ground. I
bent down to
help her up
and was amazed
at how light
she was. She

saw my questions
in my eyes
again, at what
I wanted to
ask her. She
held up a
paper thin hand,
stalling my voice.
"I am all right. Again, it is the natural way of things, these
changing of seasons."
We still walked
further along the
path of yellow
leaves. I stopped
and looked at
her closely for
the first time.
Not only was
her dress made
of leaves, but
her as well.
I could see
where the dress
should end, there
was merely the
change in colour
to a lighter
shade of leaves
that made up

her skin. I
stood back from
her, taking all
of her in.
"*Yes, I am made from leaves.*"
She said, as
if reading my
mind. She smiled.
"*It is my time to fade away. Look, there is the tree I was made
from.*"
She pointed to
a large oak
tree, it's branches
bare of all
its leaves.
She motioned to
her dress, offering
me a bright
smile. There were
tears in her
eyes though and
I longed to
wipe them away.
"*It's almost winter. That is when my time ends. I'm born when
Autumn arrives and can walk the earth when the leaves fall. My
time is almost done.*"
"**How can you stand it?**"
I asked her.

*"It is the way of things. You have to live life when it's given to you
and not spend time thinking of what could have been. You can only
think about what is."*

More of her
leaves, more
of her, fell
away as she
spoke, the leaves
joining the ones
already forming the
path. I realized
then that they
all came from
her, that she
had marked her
path across the
ground with herself.
"Why are you showing me this?"
I asked her.
She gave me
one last smile.
"So you know. So you can pass this knowledge on."
A strong breeze
ripped across the
air and her
whole form fluttered
with it, as
if she were
coming apart at

the seams. I
watched her until
all I could
see were her
eyes, blinking like
jewels among leaves.
"Don't forget. Live the life you've been given and don't look back.
Always look forward. Always."
Then a final
wind rushed by,
tearing the last
of the leaves
away. I was
surrounded by a
swirl of leaves
and could hear
the sound of
her laughter. It
was joyous, as
if she weren't
really dying. It
was the sound
of freedom. I
looked at the
path of leaves
and stopped to
pick one up.
I put it
in my pocket

and it sat
there like a
ray of sunshine
that would help
keep me warm
through the coming
winter. The wind
sounded as if
it were sighing.
"I won't forget. I promise. I won't forget."
I walked home,
thinking of the
future.

So Much Left Unsaid

There is another
half of me.
We are the
same, but dramatically
different. When we
were younger, we
spoke in our
own language. Only
we could understand
each other. Over
time, that language
was replaced by
words that everyone
could understand. As
we left behind
our own words,
our own tongue,
we grew further
apart. We stopped
hearing each other.
We stopped listening.
That doesn't mean
that I don't
carry him with
me every day
of my life.
Eighteen years have

passed since I
last spoke to
him, a whole
lifetime ago, but
he is with
me every day.
His determination and
courage are a
constant, for he
always seemed braver
than I was. Though
only fifteen minutes
separated us, I
always saw him as
my older brother
and looked up
to him. The
fact that we
no longer speak
pains me. Since
he won't hear
my voice, it
is my hope
that he will
read my words
and draw courage
and strength from
them when he
needs it most.

There is so
much I want
to say to
you, so much
I want to
tell you. We
are two sides
of the same
coin and
it is my
hope that I
can offer you
courage and strength
in return for
all you showed
me. You are
brave and have
remained a pillar
of strength for
me, even from
afar. Know that
you can do
anything you set
your mind to,
that, if you
need me, I
will be here
for you. Most
importantly, know that

I love you.
There is so
much left unsaid
but those three
words will have
to do. If
I could, I
would draw out
this new threat,
pull it from
your body. Since
I cannot, all
I can give
you is my
love and hope
that it's enough.

Silver Dreams

When I walked
into the room,
it was to
find it filled
with floating silver
orbs. A man
was standing in
the centre of
the room, regarding
me patiently. He
tilted his head
towards me and
I was struck
by how out
of place he
looked: messy blond
hair, a thin
mouth, dark sunglasses
hiding his eyes.
"What is this place?"
I asked. He
put a finger
to his chin.
"What do you want it to be?"
I shook my
head at his
bizarre answer. I

shrugged my shoulders.

"I don't know. Isn't it just a room?"

He smiled at
me and whipped
off the sunglasses.

**"Ah, but every room started out as four walls. Then they
become filled with memories and emotion. They become a
home to hearts."**

I was struck
silent for a
moment, not knowing
what to say.
He took my
silence as an
invitation to speak.

"What do you see when you look at these?"

He pointed to
the orbs floating
around the room.
The walls were
bare white and
the silver shapes
stood out starkly
against them. I
watched them floating
around the room,
bumping into one
another, only to
take a different

trajectory. I found
them oddly mesmerizing.

"They remind me of dreams."

I said softly.

"Dreams given shape, impossible to hold."

He raised his
eyebrows, clearly impressed.

"And do you have dreams? Things you wish to accomplish with your life?"

I nodded. He
smiled at me.

"Then we must let the dreams out. Dreams have no power if they aren't given flight, you know, just as a home is just walls until people live within them."

He went to
the wall and
pressed a button.
The ceiling skylights
opened very slowly.

"What are you doing?"

He smiled gently.

"They are clouds, so it's fitting that you see dreams when you look at them. Clouds are like dreams in that a person always sees something different than the last person."

"But why are you letting them out?"

"Because dreams, like clouds, must be set free. The sky is the limit after all. You must let your dreams free if you are to realize them."

The windows opened

completely and the
silver clouds, my
dreams, slipped out
into the sky.
I ran to
the centre of
the room and
watched my dreams
shining against the
blue.

A Foot Thing

He saw me
coming up the
front steps of
my apartment building.
"Hey."
He said. I
nodded at him.
"Hello."
He got up
off the front
stoop and held
the door open
for me. I
am always one
to do that
for others, but
it still surprises
me when others
do it for
me in return.
"Thank you very much."
I said. He
smiled and motioned
at my feet.
"It's no problem. You seem to have a foot thing going on there."
"A foot thing?"
I tilted my

238

head to the
right, not sure
I had heard
him correctly. He
had the good
grace to look
slightly uncomfortable, embarrassed.
"You walk funny. You had trouble coming up the stairs."
"Oh."
I said quietly.
I spend a
great deal of
time trying not
to think about
my constant companions,
disease and disability.
They are not
who I am,
what makes me,
me. They are
only a part
of who I
am and what
I can do.
"Not that it's any of my business, but why do you walk that way?"
I thought about
not answering him,
but he seemed
genuinely curious so

I answered him.

"I have Cerebral Palsy and Multiple Sclerosis."

Then I waited
for what people
usually said, the
pitying looks, words
uttered in soft
voices. Instead, he
surprised me completely.

*"Oh! Well you're doing very well then. I would never have
known."*

"Thank you."

I blushed slightly.

"I just take it one day at a time."

"Well, whatever you're doing, it's working. Keep it up."

I was warmed
by his compliment.

"Thanks,"

I said, smiling.

"I will."

I felt lighter
as I went
inside and wondered
about the difference
between how you
perceive yourself and
how others see
you.

Love Outside of Books

One night, while
I was reading,
my book began
to glow. The
pages gave off
a soft white
light. I set
the book down
and looked at
it in wonder.
A tune that
I couldn't place
played from inside
the pages. I
watched as the
words along the
page began to
reform themselves into
other words. I
watched them as
they spelled out
a message to
me. I leaned
closer to them,
but they were
a swirl of

letters I couldn't
read. The music
grew louder and
the light grew
brighter. I wasn't
afraid, but only
curious. An outline
of a hand
appeared on the
page and I
placed my hand
on it without
hesitation. The music,
so haunting and
beautiful, grew louder,
the light brighter
still until I
had to close
my eyes. When
I opened them
again, I was
inside my book,
the trees of
the Enchanted Forest
surrounding me, tall
enough to touch
the sky. In
front of me
stood the object

of my affection,
the hero of
the story. He
was even more
dashing in person.
His blond hair
flowed in the
wind and the
music that had
been coming from
the book was
louder here. He
smiled at me.
"You don't belong here."
He said. His
voice was gentle
though they uttered
a reprimand. I
nodded in agreement.
"I know I don't."
"Then why do you look for your heart's desire inside of a book?"
"Because it doesn't exist. He doesn't exist."
He shook his
head. still smiling.
"You just haven't found the right man yet. Give it time, your story still has much to be told."
"True love doesn't exist in my world. It's only in books and fairy tales that you find true love. It's why I spend so much time writing and reading."

243

He leaned forward
and ran a
thumb along my
chin. His eyes
looked deep and
serious and full
of deep warmth.

*"You have to love yourself. Only then will someone capable of true
love be able to find you."*

My skin was
warm from where
he had touched
my face. I
tried to take
in the entirety
of him, but
the light was
growing bright again.

"How will he find me?

"You shine bright like a beacon. He will find you."

"Promise?"

"As you wish."

He said. The
light grew so
bright, I had
to close my
eyes again. When
I opened them
once more, I

was back in
my own room.
"As you wish."
I repeated. I
didn't have much
luck with wishes
coming true, but
I knew this
one would. I
just had no
idea when. So
I waited and
hoped and prayed.
I got on
with my life.
I fell into
what I thought
was love when
it was something
altogether different. I
fell out of
love with myself,
believing that my
wish made all
those many years
ago would never
come true. Then
one day, I
saw a light

in the distance.
It shone brighter
than the sun,
and I was
reminded of the
light that filled
the Enchanted Forest
so long ago.
Though I tried
to get closer
to it, I
could not. I
knew that it
would come to
me in time,
or that I
would find it,
stumble upon it.
While I waited,
I focused on
myself, believing that
I would never
find the other
half of my
light, that part
of me would
remain dimmed forever.
When I had
given up hope

and had resolved
myself to being
alone for the
rest of my
life, you entered
it. I remember
the first time
I saw you,
the instant spark
that happened between
us. It created
a light that
shone so brightly
that I almost
looked away, but
I didn't. I
could only look
at you, the
shape of your
face and the
depth of your
eyes. All I
saw was kindness
and beauty and
then my light
responded to yours.
Both our beacons
intermingled until the
light became brighter,

until my body
was filled with
our glorious light.
I heard that
music of long
ago, that tune
I had heard
inside the book.
Now I realized
that it came
from me and
it was my
heart responding to
the possibility of
you. As we've
grown to know
each other, our
love and our
light has continued
to grow. You've
proved that love
doesn't exist only
inside of books
and that with
love, anything is
possible. You've proved
that wishes do
come true. I
can only give

you my heart
and watch as
our light grows
ever brighter.
"As you wish…"

Street Rat Magic

She is sitting
on the street
corner. I'm a
little surprised to
see her back.
"Irene?"
I say softly.
"What are you doing here? I thought you'd left the streets."
She looks up
at me, her eyes
wide and her
face tired and
pale. She gives
me a half
smile and shrugs.
"Times are tough, you know? Times are tough."
I want to
bend down and
give her a
hug, some sort
of comfort that
would make the
pain she carries
on her face,
in her soul,
slip away, but
I can't. Instead

I can only
give her some
form of kindness.
I take a
dollar out of
my pocket and
drop it in
her hat. She
smiles at me.
"Thanks. You were always good to me."
"It's nothing."
I tell her.
"No, when you were a street rat, you always looked out for me.
Always took care of others. I could never do that."
I smile, warmed
by her words.
As I walk
away, I reflect
at how fortunate
I am. I was
able to get
off the streets,
out of the
shelters, away from
the food banks.
Through the kindness
of others, I
found my way
back home. I

251

was lucky. However,
I know that
others aren't so
lucky, even ones
I used to
know like family.
She may not
have been family
of the blood,
but was instead
family of the
heart. She's a
street rat to
some but to
me, she will
always be a
sister. I didn't
look at what
I gave her
as just money.
In some way,
I hoped what
I was giving
her was a
bit of magic
so that she
could find her
own happily ever
after.

No Longer Broken

I went back.
Back to the
cliff, back to
where my life
had changed. I
wondered, vaguely, where
the wind had taken
the Broken Man,
that part of me
that he had
seen me as.
The most difficult
for me was
that, for a
time, I had
believe him. I
had seen myself
the same way,
until I had
set the Broken Man
free upon the
air, carried away
by the wind
to fly over
the Earth, destination
unknown. I did
wonder what had

become of him
though and was
determined to find
out. He had
been so loud
in my head
for such a
long time. I
wanted to see
what had become
of him. So
I climbed to
the top of
the cliff and
looked down into
the valley below.
I could see
water shining towards
the left of
me, feel the
air on my
face. The earth
was a rust
coloured soil that
crunched with rock
under my feet.
The sun shone
down like fire
on everything. I

looked down and
saw white stones
peppering the grass,
making a path
that led down
into the valley.
I started to
work my way
down and I
looked at each
of the stones
closely. I saw that
they were actually
the cards that
I had let
fly into the
wind that day.
The Lost Soul
was there, his
scream preserved forever
in stone. The
Forgotten One had
his back turned
to the viewers,
a crowd of
people stood around
him, small specks
of shadows. As
I made my way

further down the
mountain, some of
them spoke to
me. The Lady
of Sorrows cried
out to me:
"Stay with us! You'll be happy here in your sorrow. Remember
what was! Pain and sorrow are easier than joy!"
I moved on.
The Lord of
Treachery was
there, whispering
lies to me,
his voice like
a thick oil.
"I will give you everything. All I ask is everything in return. Of
course, I might not give you everything you want, not really."
I was on
flat ground now
and the line
of stones formed
a path that
led further along.
Each card was
a stepping stone
that I had
left behind when
I let go
of the pain,

of the hurt,
of the longing.
When I had
let those Tarot
cards from the
unknown deck fly
out of my hands,
I had instead
embraced love
embraced kindness
embraced my own
intuition. The unknown
cards all cried
out for attention.
I had already
walked this path
and chose not
to walk along
it again. I
did not step
on the stone
made from cards,
but instead regarded
everything I had
been and thought
of everything I
had become. Some
of the other
cards called out

to me. The
Knight of Knives
and Blood let
out a loud
call of joy.

"You'll never be free of us. Here, take my knife, harm yourself, let others harm you. It's what you know."

"Never."

I said softly.

"Never again."

I walked quickly
to the very
last stone in
the path, knowing
which card I
would see. There
he was, sitting
on his stone.
The Broken Man.
I regarded him
with narrowed eyes.

"You look remarkably like me."

I said. He
turned and looked
at me, smiling.

"I am you. I have always been you."

I shook my
head with vigor.

"No, you're not. You weren't me then, and you're not me now. Even at my worst, I was stronger than you."

He stood and

came towards me.

"Really? Then why am I the only card not turned to stone? Why did you return to the valley?"

I hadn't known

why, not really,

but the words

came out quickly,

as if they

had been ready,

as if they

had been waiting.

"I came for balance. I came for perspective."

"A poor place for balance, don't you think?"

I shook my

head again. He

regarded me with

narrowed eyes, dark

with intense hunger.

"Not really. It shows me what I've done, what I've left behind and everything that I've accomplished."

He laughed then,

and it was a

sound that chilled

me. His glass

legs shone as

if they were

made of diamonds
as he came
closer to me.

"You're so weak. You know you are. All it will take is one false step and you'll be back here among us."

"No, I won't."

"And why is that, pray tell?"

I regarded him
and knew that
my inner light
was shining forth.
He backed away
from me then.

"Because: you have no power over me. And I'm no longer broken."

At those words,
the legs of
The Broken Man
shattered into thousands
of pieces. His
upper body fell
to the stone
and I watched
as he began
to sink into
it, his sneer
now a grimace
of fear. I
knew how he

had felt, but
I was no
longer afraid. I
hadn't been for
some time. I
watched closely as
The Broken Man
froze completely, his
stare no longer
frightening, just sad.
The sun became
brighter around
me and I
watched as all the
stones from the
unknown Tarot deck
were wiped clean.
I looked ahead
of me and
saw other stones
were there now.
I stepped on one
and watched as
a Tarot card
appeared. I looked
down to see
what the cards
had to say.

<u>Strings</u>

There was a
red thread that
ran from my
finger and into
the air. I
often tried to
see where it
was going or
who it was
connected to, but
it was as
if the end
was made from
air, invisible to
the human eye.
It wouldn't come
off of my
finger either, but
remained stubbornly stuck
there, as if
reminding me of
something I had
forgotten. I wondered
for a while
at the purpose
of the red
thread, what it

could mean. I
started to notice
that the other
end of the
string would become
visible when I
was with someone
close to me.
I knew they
couldn't see it,
but I could,
just when they
were around me.
I started to
see other threads
in other colours
connecting everyone to
someone. The strings
were pink, purple,
blue, orange, yellow.
strings of every
colour, like a
prism hit by
light. If I
looked at the
string on my
finger in a
different light, I
realised it wasn't

just one string,
but hundreds, all
trailing from my
finger. I soon
realized how many
strings I was
tied to, how
many people I
was connected with.
I had red
strings going in
every direction, some
of them not
attached to anyone
I had met
yet. I wondered
who these strings
belonged to, who
they were. Then
I saw one
string that was
a different colour.
I hesitated only
a moment before
pulling on it.
It held strong.
It was a
deep and gorgeous
green colour. I

plucked at it
and heard the
string hum as
it vibrated. I
marveled at the
music it made.
Then I heard
another hum, felt
vibrations in my
chest where my
heart was. I
realised then that
these were heart
strings. I began
to follow that
particular heart string
to see who
it was connected
to.

Love and Light

We were in
a dark tunnel.
I knew that
I didn't want
to be there,
that there was
no light within.
You took my
hand and said:
"Don't worry. Watch what happens when I do this."
You paused for
a moment and
then you said:
"I love you."
A light flared
along the wall
of the tunnel,
showing us where
the exit lay.
We walked on
until the light
began to fade
and I clutched
your hand harder.
"You're so beautiful."
You said to
me and the

light flared again,
showing us the
way. We raced
onward until the
light began to
fade once more.
"Don't be scared."
You said softly.
"It'll be okay as long as we're together. I love you so much."
The light flared
again and under
it's blue pulse
I looked at
you, at your
beauty that shone
from the inside
out. I looked
into your eyes,
leaned in close
to kiss you.
"I love you, too."
The light increased
until it was
nearly blinding, but
we could still
see each other,
could still feel
the light we'd
created inside ourselves.

The light didn't
dim this time,
but stayed glorious,
changing from a
soft muted blue
allowing us to
see in the
dark into a
light so wonderful,
so pure, it
was like we
had created the
sun. You took
hold of my
hand and led
me out of
the tunnel and
towards the future.

When Words Aren't Necessary

There are times
when we don't
even need to
speak, when words
aren't necessary. Every
gesture is inductive
of words that
don't need to
be spoken aloud.
When we're going
down the stairs,
he gives me
his arm. With
that action, he
tells me silently:
"I'll support you."
When I lose
my balance and
he catches me,
he's really whispering:
"I got you."
When he holds
my hand in
public while we
walk down the
street, what he's
really saying is:

"I'm proud to be with you."
When he reads
something I've written
and sees me
inside the words,
what he's really saying is
"I know you."
And when he
holds me close,
his heart beating
so close to
mine, what he's
really saying is:
"I love you."
Though I don't
have to tell
him, to utter
what he already
knows, I do.
"I love you, too."

We Are Our Passions

"How's your writing going?"
I told him
that I was
halfway through
my current novel,
that I had
written a bunch
of poems and
short stories. He
nodded, looking serious.
"I don't see how you can write so much. You're always going out."
He was a
person that lived
in my building,
but he was
also a photographer.
I shrugged nonchalantly.
"Well, I have to go to work. It pays the bills."
He looked smug
for a second
before he said:
"So you're not a writer."
"I'm sorry?"
I was confused.
"What do you mean?"
His look of

smugness intensified and

he actually laughed.

"Well, anyone that doesn't support themselves with their writing is not a writer. It's merely a hobby."

I was stunned

at his rudeness.

"Do you support yourself with your photography?"

If possible, he

looked even more

smug. His smile

was like a

streak of oil

across his face.

"I do actually."

"And how's that working out for you?"

His smile faltered

a little bit.

"I do well enough."

He said, but

there was a

bluster to his

statement. I looked

him right in

the eye, not

backing down from

his smug stare.

"Let me make something perfectly clear. Whether or not I support myself with my writing doesn't make me any less of a

writer. The same goes for all artists, musicians and even photographers."

"Yes, but-"

I cut him
off. I didn't
want to hear
anything else he
had to say.

"Writing is what I'm most passionate about. It's how I live, how I breathe, how I survive. That is why I'm a writer, through and through. And you know what? It's only a matter of time before I am doing what I love for a living."

I watched him
deflate a little
bit, a stooping
of the shoulders.
I walked away
from him and
went back into
my apartment to
do what I
love most and
with every word
I put down
on paper, I
found more of
myself waiting there
to bleed through
the page.

Doorways and Starlight

I woke in
darkness. I got
out of bed
and walked toward
a rectangle of
light that shone
in the distance.
I knew that
if I opened
the door, there
would be brightness
to chase away
the dark. I
opened the door
and stepped through
the doorway. I
found myself in
a place I
used to know.
I had called
it home, though
towards the end,
it did not
fill me with
a feeling of
peace as homes
are supposed to

do. The walls
of places we
have known retain
voices of the
past, vibrations of
sound lost in
concrete and plaster.
I put my
hand on one
of the walls
and felt the
sadness there, the
turmoil. I took
my hand away
and looked at
my palm. It
was red, as
if it had
been burned. I
ran towards another
doorway and stepped
through it. I
found myself in
another place I
had called home
but it had
just been another
way station. The
walls here looked

as if they
were crying, thick
tears like wax
were seeping out
of the walls.
If the previous
place had held
sound, this one
held emotion. I
had tried to
find myself here
but to no
avail. I had
only found heartache.
I went to
the doorway to
the sun-room and
could see the
sky shining through
the cracks. I
opened the door
and stepped through
it. I was
inside my dark
basement apartment. I
had known despair
here, heartache and
disaster. However, oddly
enough, I had

found myself here,
had realized what
I was truly
capable of inside
these walls. In
the darkest part
of my life,
I had found
myself. I stepped
forward and placed
my hand on
the rough walls.
Instead of emotion
or sound, I
saw myself as
I had been.
I lay in
my bed, the
stories I longed
to tell brought
to life above
me as if
they were dreams
given life. I
could see characters
I had created
living out their
destinies and I
lay there, powerless

to stop the
story from going
forward. I watched
as I found
the strength to
learn to walk
once more, the
will to move
forward, the courage
to continue. It
was here that,
instead of giving
up, as I
had been tempted
to do, I
chose to live
instead. If the
previous places had
held sound and
emotion, this one
housed my strength
until I was
strong enough to
accept it. I could
hear music, a
soft kaleidoscope of
notes coming from
another doorway. I
stepped through it

eager to leave
the darkness behind.
I opened the
door into the
hallway and stepped
through into light.
I was in
my current place,
the first one
that felt like
home instead of
just a place
to exist. However,
the music wasn't
coming from here.
These walls were
bathed in light,
but the music
came from somewhere
further on. I
felt as if
I was standing
on a precipice
as I stood in
front of the doorway
of my apartment.
This place held
light within its
walls. I wondered

what would come
next? I reached
out a hand
and opened the
door. I heard
the kaleidoscope of
music, louder this
time, but could
see only stars.
I stood at
the doorway wondering
what to do,
when I heard
his lovely voice.
"You're perfect for me. You complete me. I love you."
The music around
me swelled to
a loud crescendo
and I stepped
through the doorway
and into starlight,
waiting to feel
his arms around
me. As I
fell through the
stars, I marveled
at the fact
that it had
taken finding myself

to find the
other half of
my heart.

Growing Invisible Light

"What's wrong with you today?"
I looked up.
A friend was
looking at me
with worried concern.
"What do you mean?"
"Well, you just don't seem to be here today. Like you're lost in your head."
"I haven't had coffee yet."
She shrugged and
made a face.
"It's more than that. It's like you're not really here."
I shrugged and
went on with
my day. At
first, I didn't
pay her words
any attention. However,
when my fingers
began to slide
into the keyboard
instead of hitting
the keys, I
wondered. Looking at
my fingers, I
noticed that they
had grown dim,

there, but not.
I could see
the outline of
them, I could
feel them, but
they weren't visible.
She came over
to me again
and looked closely
at me with
growing concern. Reaching
out, she touched
my face with
soft, careful fingers.
"What's wrong with your skin? It's clear."
"Clear how?"
"Like, it's like your face is made of glass."
I ran to
the washroom and
looked in the
mirror. I saw
that she was
telling the truth.
The skin of
my face had
gone dim, indeed
clear as glass.
I wondered if,
somehow, I was

growing invisible. I
finished my day,
wondering if more
of me would
cease to exist
by the days'
end. There was
a heat growing
in my stomach.
It pulsed inside
of me and
I could feel
it snaking its
way further inside
my body with
each pulse. I
left the building
and stumbled outside.
The skies were
grey and the
air cold. Snow
was falling down
like fairy dust.
The heat growing
in me pulsed
again and despite
myself, I cried
out loud, heedless
of people looking.

"What's happening to me?"

An older woman
stopped and looked
at me. She
smiled kindly at
me and came
closer. She held
out her hand
and touched my
face. I was
astounded to see
wetness on her
fingers and wondered
when I had
started crying. She
gave me another
kind, beautiful smile.

"Don't you know? This is your first time isn't it?"

I shook my
head. I didn't
know what she
was talking about.

"The first time?"

"You're letting your light shine. I can see it there inside you."

"You can?"

"Yes. It's so bright, I can hardly look at you, but I want to."

"I don't understand."

She smiled again.

"Well, look around you. Only grey, cold skies. People need light. Didn't your mother ever tell you that you were a light bringer?"

"I don't know what that is."

"That pulse inside you? Let it out, set it free."

"But my body…"

"Will go back to the way it was afterwards. Here, I'll shine with you."

She took my
hand and I
watched as the
opaqueness of her
skin faded and
she too was
as there and
not there as
I was. She
smiled at me.

"Come on now, let it out. Shine bright, little sun."

I watched as
her own light
began to shine,
first a growing
sliver of sunlight,
then a blinding
flash of brightness.
My own light
responded in kind
and the pulse
thickened, intensified, grew.

The light shone
from me as
if it was
always meant to
do so, filling
the skies, once
grey and dreary,
with bright and
beautiful sunlight. It
streamed from me,
from the woman
beside me, and
I could hear
music, as if
a choir was
singing around us.
As quickly as
it had come,
the light faded.
I stood there,
holding the woman's
hand. I could
see my fingers
again, could see
hers. The smile
I wore on
my face was
like its own
kind of light.

"Thank you."
I said. She
smiled once more.
"No thanks needed. I just gave you the push you needed. There's
so much light in you. You have to share it every once in a while."
As she started
to walk away,
the snow began
to fall in
heavier, thicker flakes.
I called after her.
"Will I see you again?"
She turned back
and smiled again.
"Just let your light shine. I'll see it wherever I am."
She turned again
and walked away
and was soon
lost in the
falling snow. I
stood there, the
pulse still moving
through me. I
was happier than
I had been
in a long
time. I looked
to where her
silhouette was still

walking farther away.

"Shine bright."

I said.

When Goodbye Becomes Goodnight

It's hard to sleep
at night when half
of my heart is not
beside me.
I find it difficult
to take in a full breath,
when he is not
with me.
Every time he leaves,
saying goodbye when
the night comes
to an end,
I watch half
of my heart walk
out of the door.
I wish that I could
control time so that
I could speed it up
to the moment that
we're able to live together.
Then I think of all
the wonderful times
with him that I would
miss if time was
under my control.
So, instead, I will
simply have to remain

patient for the moment
that the two halves
of my heart are reunited and
goodbye becomes goodnight.

A Path of Sunlight

The path that
I used to
walk on was
one filled with
darkness and shadows.
 It had gotten
to a point
where I could
recognize them
and knew some
of them so
well that they
had almost become
friends. I could
recognize their shapes,
their movements. The
path was rocky
and filled with
pieces of glass
that cut my
feet. Still, I
walked along the
path, as it
was mine to
walk, alone. The
skies were filled

with clouds and
still more shadows,
rain a constant
threat. I could
see the sun
peeking through from
time to time,
but it would
never last for
very long. Then
I came to
a turn in
the path, a
different direction from
where I had
been going, and
you were standing
there, waiting for
me, your hand
outstretched waiting to
clasp mine. When
I put my
hand in yours,
the clouds cleared,
grass began to
sprout through the
rough soil and
the sunshine shone
so brightly. I

looked around me
and the whole
world looked different.
When I looked
inside me, I
didn't recognize myself.
You have not
only transformed my
world into something
beautiful, you have
transformed me as
well with your
love for me.
The path ahead
of me is filled
with sunlight as
long as I
walk beside you
and we walk
together towards the
future.

About the Author

Jamieson is an award winning, author of over sixty books including the Number One Best Seller, Talking to the Sky.

He is also an accomplished artist. He works in mixed media, charcoal, pastels and oil paints.

He currently lives in Ottawa, Ontario, Canada with his cat, Tula, who is fearless.

Learn more about Jamieson at www.JamiesonWolf.com

www.ingramcontent.com/pod-product-compliance
Lightning Source LLC
LaVergne TN
LVHW022321080426
835508LV00041B/1605